D1015352

Always Abounding

The Way To Prosper In Good Times, Bad Times, Any Time

by

John Avanzini

Harrison House
Tulsa, Oklahoma

Always Abounding —
The Way to Prosper in
Good Times, Bad Times, Any Time
ISBN 0-89274-581-9
Copyright © 1989 by Dr. John Avanzini
Box 1057
Hurst, Texas 76053

Published by Harrison House, Inc.
P. O. Box 35035
Tulsa, OK 74153

Dedication

This book is
lovingly dedicated to
Paul and Jan Crouch
of the
Trinity Broadcasting Network

Contents

1

Give — Expecting To Receive

Every time God shows me something in the Scriptures that shatters man's normal way of thinking, my first reaction is shock. Not long ago when I was helping in a telethon, I received just such a shock.

Kenny Forman was delivering a message, and he made a statement that stirred my spirit. Kenny said: "It is God's way of giving. . .to give, expecting to receive something for the gift. It is a *godly way* to give to expect something for what you give!"

Those words really jarred my entire system. His statements were exactly backwards from everything I had ever been taught. Every teacher who ever had an impact on my life had taught me I should give, but never expect anything in return for my gift.

My mother and father had taught me that. All of my school teachers had taught me that. Bible college professors had taught me that. Everyone had taught me this very same principle — not the principle Forman taught, but the exact opposite.

They taught me *never* to expect something back from something I gave. How could it be *godly* to expect something back from my gifts to God?

When I began to study and search the Scriptures on this topic, how different I found the teachings and truths of God to be from the errors of man. Your Creator has always given, *expecting* to receive something in return!

In the very beginning, God created man out of the dust of the earth. He breathed into man the great gift of life — God's second gift. But when God gave man life, He was *expecting to receive* something back for the gift. God was expecting man to give Him worship, reverence, love, service, and obedience.

And if that first example of God giving, expecting to receive, starts to strip the cobwebs off your traditional ideas, then begin to digest the power of this thought: God's greatest gift of all, his most precious Son, Jesus Christ, was given by God with an expectation!

When God sent Jesus Christ to the earth, He wanted something *back* from man. He *expected to receive* men and women who would become His children.

Let this truth soak into your spirit: Expecting to receive something in return is a godly way to give.

The truth is often shocking. You are probably saying: "Why, Brother John, that thought just goes against all I've been taught, all that I know about how a good Christian gives to others!"

Now is the time for you to stop thinking man's thoughts. Learn now to hear God's Word, and think God's thoughts without putting a short circuit in your mind. If the Bible clearly teaches *anything*, it teaches to *give, expecting to receive*.

Ask the Holy Spirit right now to remove the spiritual blinders and to help you see Luke 6:38 in a fresh way. You have read it many times before, but this time read it with the anointed eyes of truth.

Give, and it shall be given unto you; good measure, pressed down and shaken together, and running over, shall men give into your bosom. For with the same measure that ye mete (measure) **withal it shall be measured to you again.**

I believe God is working on your spirit right now, and that you are beginning to understand His Word for you. Now look at what God says in Malachi 3:10. He says that when you tithe, He will ...**open you the windows of heaven, and pour you out a blessing.**

See what God says in Galatians 6:7: **Be not deceived; God is not mocked: for whatsoever a man soweth, that shall he also reap.**

Give, expecting to receive. Expecting to receive something in return is a godly way to give.

If you have financial needs, if you are sitting there staring at a stack of overdue bills, if you need something *from* God, then give something *to* God.

If your house payment is past due, and you are wondering what to do, the Word tells you this: Today, this very day, give something back to the Lord. Give, and it shall be given back to you.

I started this chapter with a shocking statement, so it is only appropriate that I should also end it with one. If you are currently experiencing a tight financial situation in your life, it is very likely that you have not been giving enough away — to God.

"But Brother John, that just doesn't make good sense!" shouts the Skeptic. You are right. It might not make good sense, but it certainly makes *God* sense. Read what God says in Isaiah 55:8,9:

> **For my thoughts are not your thoughts, neither are your ways my ways, saith the Lord.**
>
> **For as the heavens are higher than the earth, so are my ways higher than your ways, and my thoughts than your thoughts.**

In God's world, the first shall be last. In God's world, the leader must be the servant of all. In God's world, you must give away what you want in order to receive it. If you want to receive from God, you must first give to Him.

Paul understood this principle of giving to receive when he wrote in Philippians 4:15-17:

> **Now ye Philippians know also, that in the beginning of the gospel, when I departed from Macedonia, no church communicated with me as concerning giving and receiving, but ye only.**
>
> **For even in Thessalonica ye sent once and again unto my necessity.**
>
> **Not because I desire a gift: but I desire fruit that may abound to your account.**

Paul understood the principle: expecting to receive is a godly way to give.

He felt concerned when those he loved failed to apply God's principle in their lives. Paul knew the result of the application was fruit to their account.

Every time God speaks in His Word about giving, He also speaks about what He will do as a result. Tithe, and the windows of heaven will open. Give, and it shall be given unto you.

Let this message sink into your spirit: expecting to receive is a godly way to give.

2
You Can Bank on His Promises

Whenever I write about giving, somebody gets angry. But the one person who never gets angry when I write about money and giving is God. He is glad when I write about giving. He knows it is only when you give that He can begin to release His wealth back to you to meet your needs.

If there were some thoughts in the last chapter that shook some of the shackles from your traditional thinking, then look at 2 Corinthians 9:6-11 in *The Living Bible* which contains a principle so powerful it will stagger you. Read this passage and make it part of your thought process, and it will change your life!

But remember this — if you give little, you will get little. A farmer who plants just a few seeds will get only a small crop, but if he plants much, he will reap much.

Every one must make up his own mind as to how much he should give. Don't force anyone to give more than he really wants to, for cheerful givers are the ones God prizes.

God is able to make it up to you by giving you everything you need and more, so that there will not only be enough for your own needs, but plenty left over to give joyfully to others.

It is as the Scriptures say: 'The godly man gives generously to the poor. His good deeds will be an honor to him forever.'

> For God, who gives seed to the farmer to plant, and later on, good crops to harvest and eat, will give you more and more seed to plant and will make it grow so that you can give away more and more fruit from your harvest.
>
> Yes, God will give you much so that you can give away much....

What powerful verses of scripture!

Begin now to grasp the significance of this principle. God tells you He will give you much fruit so you can "give away more" from your harvest. So often this part is not stressed in teachings about giving. Givers *do* get, according to the Bible. But they get to *give again to His work*! God wants to entrust His wealth to those who will wisely "give away more" for His purposes. When you plant seed money in the gospel ministry, into His fields for His work, then He promises it will bring forth a great harvest.

When a farmer puts a seed in the ground, he does not get back just one seed. He puts that seed into the earth, the seed produces a stalk of corn, the stalk produces an ear of corn, and that ear produces hundreds of new seeds — all from one seed the farmer planted!

That is why God is able to give you ... **everything you need and more** (v. 8).

"But Brother John," you say, "I simply cannot give to God. I have too many immediate and pressing needs."

Quit listening to that old man. Quit listening to the devil whispering in your ear about scant rations, about doing without. What does God say?

He tells you to plant your money in His work, in the Gospel of our Lord and Savior, Jesus Christ. He tells you that if you will give to His work, then He will give you everything you need and more.

Many of His people this very day are beginning to catch the vision of being bankers for God. They have learned that they literally cannot give too much away when they give in the name of the Lord. Each time they give an offering, and are in the will of God, He uses it for His purposes, and returns it multiplied to them to give again in greater abundance for His purposes.

The cycle continues to grow, because we cannot outgive God, no matter how we try.

During these times of economic chaos and unpredictable money markets, these "spiritual bankers" have found the secret to God's abundance, and they now *bank* on God, *bank* on His promises, and look to no other earthly bank for their source.

By now the Spirit of God is already working on you as you read this book; you are not reading it by accident. I believe God wants you to know and understand His Biblical principles so you can begin to apply them in your life, and so He can begin to bless you in your giving to Him. In fact, He cannot bless you financially until, by your gift, you first release Him to act. You must first give, so He can return back to you.

This "release process" applies not only to money, but to any area of your life. Every day, spiritual forces of faith and fear fight on the battlefield of your mind and spirit. You are constantly faced with decisions to *trust God* and His promises in faith, or to function in fear apart from His promises.

Every day you make a choice: either you exercise *faith* and *feast* in the abundance of God's supply, or you give in to the devil and *fear*, and suffer personal *famine*.

In Genesis 26, God's servant Isaac fought the same battle. There was a famine in his land. The ground was dry. Isaac had a need, but there was seemingly, no answer in sight. *Fearful* he would starve if he stayed in Israel, Isaac decided to go into Egypt to avoid the famine.

In this situation, Egypt and Israel are symbolic for your life. Egypt stood for the world and man's ability. Israel stood for God — His ability, His supply. God warned Isaac not to go into Egypt! In fact, God instructed Isaac not only to *stay* in the land, but *He instructed him to sow in the midst of famine, in the midst of hunger, and in the midst of drought.*

Now, Isaac had to make a decision. He could ignore God, give in to his fear, see only the circumstances of drought and famine, or he could see beyond his circumstances, exercise *faith*, and be obedient to God.

He chose to stay in the land and sow. He chose to obey God. He chose faith over fear, obedience to God's promises over fear.

Do you know that before God prospered Isaac, Isaac had to do one more thing? He had to put his *faith* into *action*!

He had to sow seeds — precious seeds. Never are seeds more precious and valuable than in a time of famine, a time of personal need.

By his actions, Isaac released the power of God in his life. The Word records that Isaac did sow, in the midst of drought, and God blessed him a hundredfold — in the same year! (Genesis 16:12.)

Your choice is the same as Isaac's. *You can release the power of God* to meet the needs in your life. The example of Isaac provides two vital keys:

1. Choose *faith* over *fear,* and

2. Exercise your *faith* — bank on God's promises by your *action.*

Read Ecclesiastes 11:1-6. It not only says to **cast thy bread upon the waters: for thou shalt find it after many days** (v. 1), it also says, **He that observeth the wind shall not sow; and he that regardeth the clouds shall not reap** (v. 4).

Now is the time to take your eyes off your circumstances. If you are in famine, take your eyes off your fears. Put your faith in God's promises into action, and sow in your time of famine.

God is faithful, and as you act, He will multiply your action back to you. God wants to make a mighty witness of your faithfulness, just as He did with Isaac.

Nothing can stop God's promises, except *you.* Please do not misunderstand me here. God is all powerful; He can do all things. But this is His principle: You must act before God is free to bless your action.

Isaac could have stopped the flow of God's abundance and supply simply by refusing to act, simply by refusing to sow his precious seed. If Isaac had decided to hoard his precious seed, he would have starved.

The world teaches: "Hide your treasures; times are hard. Get all you can; can all you get; then guard the can."

The *Word* teaches: **They that sow in tears shall reap in joy** (Ps. 126:5).

When do you sow in tears? When the seed is precious, when the times are hard! These are not my words; these are not my ideas; they are from the Word of God.

You can *bank* on His promises.

3

Today's Taboo Topic — Tithing

By now your spirit is starting to grasp the necessity of giving so you can free God to act in your life with His abundant blessings.

You are convinced you need to plant seed in order to begin to reap a harvest, and are now asking: "Well, Brother John, just how much seed money do you think I should plant? Don't forget, I've got the house payment coming due, and there are three other payments in the next two weeks. So, go easy on me, OK?"

If you listen to the Word, your life will be easier. Read Malachi 3:8:

> **Will a man rob God? Yet ye have robbed me. But ye say, Wherein** (how) **have we robbed thee?...**

Look at the answer:

> **...In *tithes* and offerings.**

Tithing is the first step toward receiving from God.

For some strange reason, tithing seems to be today's taboo topic. In their eagerness to talk about a loving and gentle God, preachers seem to want to avoid the clear but strict requirement God has for His faithful stewards.

Many would have you believe tithing is not for today. *Tithing is for today*!

Many preachers feel tithing is too legalistic, and that it has to do with the Law. Tithing is *not* from the

Law. In Hebrews 7:1-10, we see that Abraham (before the Law) paid tithes. He not only paid tithes for himself, but he paid tithes for Levi, who did live under the dispensation of the Law.

We are Abraham's seed. Galatians 3:7 tells us that they that are Christ's are Abraham's seed. Abraham tithed for all of his posterity: for his natural seed, for his seed that lived before the Law and during the Law, and for his seed that now lives in the dispensation of grace. Tithing reached across the lines of the pre-law period and the patriarchal period. Then it extended into the Levitical era and it went on into the era of grace in which we live today.

Jesus approved of tithing.

In Matthew 23:23, referring to the Pharisees who had tithed in mint, cummin, and anise, Jesus made the statement, **These ought ye to have done** [judgment, mercy, faith] **and not to leave the other undone** (speaking of the tithe). This Scripture indicates very clearly that tithing is for our day.

Many Christians believe the tithe is discretionary and that they can tithe whenever the mood hits them. But we saw earlier that to fail to tithe is to rob God. Read further what God says happens when you fail to meet your obligation to Him.

Ye are cursed with a curse: for ye have robbed me, even this whole nation.

Bring ye all the tithes into the storehouse, that there may be meat (food) **in mine house, and prove** (test) **me now herewith, saith the Lord of hosts, if I will not open you the windows of heaven, and pour**

you out a blessing, that there shall not be room enough to receive it.

And I will rebuke the devourer for your sakes, and he shall not destroy the fruits of your ground; neither shall your vine cast its fruit before the time in the field, saith the Lord of hosts.

Malachi 3:9-11

Feel and understand God's Spirit in this. He warns His people not to take from Him what is His — do not rob Him. Instead He tells us to bring in tithes. Why? So He can make us poor? So He can see to it that we miss our next house payment? So He can watch our children miss the next several meals?

No! So He can open for us the windows of heaven.

Christianity goes through teaching cycles. Before the subject of tithing became taboo, preachers used to teach it as something you *must* do out of obedience, out of painful necessity.

But read *His Word*! Once again, we see that the teachings of man often do not capture the spirit of the Scriptures.

God does not ask you to tithe to punish you, to make things hard. God wants you to tithe *so He can bless you*.

Grasp the totality of God's will for you. Tithe, so He can *open the windows of heaven, and pour out for you a blessing*.

During the time of Jesus, the government did not withhold taxes from paychecks. Many children of God come to me and ask: "Brother John, do I tithe on my income *before* I pay my taxes or *after* I pay them?"

Let Jesus answer that question for you. Read Luke 20:25:

And he said unto them, Render therefore unto Caesar the things which be Caesar's, and unto God the things which be God's.

You decide who has top priority in your life. Does the government have first place, or does the Lord have top priority? Can you give the Lord the first fruits of your harvest if you have already given away the taxes? I believe if you think and pray about this matter, you will find that Caesar — that is, the government — certainly does not have priority over the Lord. The first fruits should not go to Caesar, but to the Lord God Almighty.

Once you have decided that you need to tithe in order for God to bless you, and you accept that you will give one-tenth of your income, before taxes, toward His work, you still have another question to answer. Where do you tithe?

Again, let's look at the Scriptures. They say to bring your tithe ...**into the storehouse, that there may be** (food) **meat in mine house....**

I believe the Bible clearly teaches that you bring it to your spiritual storehouse, the place where you receive your meat. If you belong to a good, Bible-teaching, Bible-preaching, meat-producing church — a place where you are getting fed — then you should bring your tithe into that place; that is your storehouse.

But here is a problem many people face. What if you do not belong to a good, gospel-preaching church? What if there is not one in your local community? What if there is not a local church where the meat of God is being distributed?

Pastors, please do not become upset with me. I, too, have been a pastor. I pastored a church more than 25 years.

But, if there is not a meat-giving house of God in your local community, then give where you receive your meat. Maybe you are a shut-in, and have no access to a meat-giving church. It is very possible that your meat comes from a television ministry or from a book or tape ministry. Then you should tithe to that ministry.

Pay careful attention to what I say about this. I am not advocating sending your tithes to some other organization if you are in a gospel-preaching church. But there are thousands upon thousands upon thousands *who need the benefit* of tithing — who need to have the windows of heaven open in their lives — yet there is no local assembly where the meat of God is distributed to them.

If that is true of you, I suggest you put your tithe in an envelope and follow the Bible's instructions. Send it to the storehouse from which you are receiving spiritual nourishment.

4

With the Same Measure

With great sorrow, I make this next statement. *Most Christians do not tithe*! For many years I was confused as to the reason for this miserable showing. For a while I thought it was because non-tithers did not love God. Experience has caused me to change my mind about this.

Since traveling worldwide and meeting millions of God's children, I am now convinced there is another reason. Most have simply been misinformed as to what the Bible actually promises the tither.

The majority of non-tithers are in disobedience because of one simple reason. Their problem has been caused by what the *King James Version* of the Bible teaches in Malachi.

> **Bring ye all the tithes into the storehouse, that there may be meat in mine house, and prove me now herewith, saith the Lord of hosts, if I will not open you the windows of heaven, and pour you out a blessing, that *there shall* not *be room* enough *to receive it*.**
>
> **Malachi 3:10**

This promise has never taken place. I am not saying God makes a promise He won't keep. Neither am I saying the Word of God is not accurate. What I am saying is that the *King James Version* does not translate Malachi 3:10 accurately.

Please think this through with me. Have you ever met a tither who was receiving so much that he could not receive any more? You and I know the honest answer to that question is *No*! There are no tithers who have to turn down money or possessions because they have no more room to receive them.

Actually, the very opposite of this is true. All the tithers I know or have ever heard of are not only capable of receiving much more from God, but they are actually expecting more from God.

In all honesty we must conclude that something is desperately wrong with the translation of this verse.

I must confess, I silently pondered the inconsistency of this verse for many years. Then one day, just as if a light had been turned on, God showed me the answer to the problem. It was the *King James Version* that made it possible for me to detect the error.

The way the *King James Version* of the Bible is written is of immeasurable help to the serious Bible student. It has a code in it to alert the informed reader of any deviation from the exact words of the original manuscript. Every word in the translation that does not appear in the original language is *always* printed in *italics*. This allows the reader to instantly identify the word the translator has added to clarify the original text. It is a universally accepted rule of Bible interpretation that when a word is italicized in the *King James Version*, it can be omitted without losing the meaning of the original text.

If you have not noticed, please notice now. Malachi 3:10 is one of the most italicized verses of scripture in the entire *King James Version* of the Bible. Seven of the last ten words are in italics.

> ...that *there shall* **not** *be room* **enough** *to receive it.*
>
> **Malachi 3:10**

Notice how the meaning of the verse is completely changed with the removal of these seven words. With the italicized words in place, the text erroneously says that the tither will be given a blessing in so much abundance that there will not be room to receive it all. However, when these italicized words are omitted, the verse tells us when we open the windows of heaven with our tithe, it is not enough. After the tithe is given, there is still more for the tither to do.

Look at the entire tenth verse again, but this time do not look at it with the traditional understanding. Look at it with your spirit open, allowing God to form His thoughts in your hearts.

> **Bring ye all the tithes into the storehouse, that there may be meat in mine house, and prove me now herewith, saith the Lord of hosts, if I will not open you the windows of heaven, and pour you out a blessing that not enough.**
>
> **Malachi 3:10**

If you look closely, you will see that it is the Lord's house, not our house, that will be filled with meat (abundant supply) by our tithe.

> ...that there may be meat in *mine house*.

See how our traditions tend to make the Word of God of *no effect*.

In this book, italics are primarily used to show emphasis. Please refer to the *King James Version* text for the exact words italicized by its writers.

> **Making the Word of God of none effect through your tradition. . . .**
>
> **Mark 7:13**

The plain teaching of the Scriptures is that God is not obliged to give anything to anyone until something has been given to Him.

> *Give*, **and it shall be given unto you; good measure, pressed down, and shaken together, and running over, shall men give into your bosom. For with the same measure that ye mete withal** *it shall be measured to you again.*
>
> **Luke 6:38**

Most Christians make the mistake of considering their tithe as a *gift* to God. According to the Bible, the tithe *belongs* to God. Those who tithe are simply returning to the Lord that which is already His.

> *. . .all the tithe* **of the land. . .** *is the Lord's*; **it is holy unto the Lord.**
>
> **Leviticus 27:30**

Not only does the tithe belong to the Lord, but it is clearly stated that it must be returned to Him in a timely manner. If not, He charges the delinquent tither a *very high interest rate.*

> **And if a man will at all redeem aught** (hold back any) **of his tithes, he shall add thereto the** *fifth part* (20%) **thereof.**
>
> **Leviticus 27:31**

There it is in black and white. The tithe is the Lord's, and it must not be kept back from Him. If it is, God charges twenty percent interest!

Let this sink down into your spirit. God does not owe anyone so much that **there shall not be room**

enough to receive it when they tithe. The tithe is His already.

Realizing this, let me help you to see just what giving the tithe does for us. *It opens the windows of heaven.*

It is a universal practice among men to close and lock the windows and doors to keep thieves out of the house. Is it any surprise to find that God does this same thing? As long as a person robs God of the tithe, the windows of heaven stay tightly closed over his life. While the windows of heaven are closed, the increase of God is blocked.

Look again at God's promise to open the windows of heaven over your life each time you faithfully tithe.

> **Bring ye all the tithes into the storehouse, that there may be meat in mine house, and prove me now herewith, saith the Lord of hosts,** *if I will not open you the windows of heaven, and pour you out a blessing....*
> **Malachi 3:10**

Every time you tithe, the windows of heaven open. God then stands ready to *pour* out a blessing. But remember our three important words, *that not enough*. Something more is needed. God says it is not enough to simply open the windows of heaven with your tithe. Everything in heaven won't just start tumbling out through those windows. The blessings must be *poured out*.

The words *poured out* speak of a measured amount. In Ferrar Fenton's translation of this verse, he refers to the windows of heaven as the sluice of heaven. A sluice is a special water gate used to measure specific amounts of water from a reservoir. It allows water to be measured out to the community according to the portion it has invested into the reservoir.

God does not *pour out* the same amount of blessings to everyone who tithes. Each tither must establish the measure God is to use.

Go back with me to Malachi 3:8 and notice the last words of the verse.

> ...Wherein have we robbed thee? In *tithes and offerings.*
>
> **Malachi 3:8**

Here is the missing key. God is reporting a two-fold robbery. There is not just a robbery of the tithe, but there is also a robbery of *offerings.*

The measure of the blessing God can pour out is always established by the measure of your offerings.

Look with me again at God's greatest offering scripture:

> **Give, and it shall be given unto you**...*for with the same measure that ye mete withal it shall be measured to you again.*
>
> **Luke 6:38**

Your tithe *opens* the windows of heaven. Your offering *determines the measure* God can use to bless you. If you give your offerings with an *eyedropper*, you have bound the hand of God to bless you with an *eyedropper.*

Whatever measure you use when you give to God, He is bound by His Word to use that same measure when He gives to you.

If you use a *teaspoon*, God must use a teaspoon to bless you. If you give offerings to God by the *cupful*,

He will joyfully be able to bless you by the *cupful*. This principle works *right up to the train load and beyond*.

Let me encourage you to begin giving with this new understanding for just six months. If you do, you will never stop. Begin by returning the tithe to God from every increase. Then add to this a *generous offering*.

The missing ingredient in the lives of most tithers is the offering. When the tithe is faithfully given, and the offering is generous, then Luke 6:38 will be fully realized.

> *For with the same measure that ye mete withal it shall be measured to you again.*
>
> **Luke 6:38**

In case there are any who do not believe it is proper to omit the seven italicized words in the *King James Version* of Malachi 3:10, I would like to suggest you check the following accepted translations of this verse.

The Berkeley Version

The Jerusalem Bible

The Douay Version

The New English Bible

Ferrar Fenton's Version

You will find that none of these say there will be a blessing so great **that there shall not be room enough to receive it.**

5
Six Steps to a Proper Offering

Before you can decide the right amount of money to give in an offering, you must know there is a definite difference between your tithe and your offering. Remember, the tithe is not a gift to God. Neither is it a part of your offering to God. The Scriptures say the tithe is always the Lord's property. When you pay the tithe on your increase, you are simply returning to God the portion of your income that already belongs to Him.

> . . .*All the tithe* **of the land, whether of the seed of the land, or of the fruit of the tree,** *is the Lord's: it is holy unto the Lord.*
>
> **Leviticus 27:30**

There should not be any difficulty determining the amount of your tithe. The Hebrew word *tithe* literally means "tenth," and the Scriptures clearly show that the tithe is ten percent of your increase. The Bible confirmation of this can be found by comparing the following verses of scripture:

> . . .**And he** (Abraham) **gave him** (Melchizedek) *tithes* **of all.**
>
> **Genesis 14:20**

> (Melchizedek) **To whom also Abraham gave a** *tenth part* **of all. . . .**
>
> **Hebrews 7:2**

Without question the tithe is ten percent. All Christians should give ten percent of their income to the Lord each time they are paid, or any time they receive an increase.

The offerings are a totally different matter.

> **Will a man rob God? Yet ye have robbed me. But ye say, Wherein have we robbed thee? In tithes *and offerings.***
>
> **Malachi 3:8**

Every Christian is required to give offerings, according to this verse.

A proper understanding of this chapter will greatly increase the return you experience from your giving. You will learn to let God guide you in giving the amount He desires you to give.

It should not be supposed that every offering will be the same dollar amount. Each time an offering is given, it must be considered as a separate event.

Many Christians make the mistake of setting a standard amount to give for certain types of offerings. For instance, they might give $20 to every visiting evangelist, $30 to every missionary, exactly $5 each week for Sunday School, and so on. This is an easy habit to fall into. It is also a very destructive one. Realizing the exact amount God wants you to give in each offering is of the utmost importance to you. As you learn to discern His will when you give, you will find yourself participating in the full abundance of God.

After 31 years of Bible study, most of which have been spent in the area of Biblical economics, I have found six simple steps that will help guide you in determining the amount you should give in each offering. If you faithfully follow these steps, I can say with confidence that you will always know exactly how much God wants you to give.

Step One: *You must have a willing mind.*

If you are not of a willing mind, it is impossible for God to guide you. God never drives His children. It is always the devil who tries to drive us. God always *leads* His children. As long as your mind is not willing, you cannot give a proper offering.

In one of his letters to the Corinthians, the Apostle Paul stated that willingness was a requirement for giving a proper offering.

> **For if there be first a willing mind....**
> **2 Corinthians 8:12**

Proper giving always begins with a *willing mind*. The greatest offering ever recorded in the Bible was given when only the willing-hearted were allowed to participate.

> **Take ye from among you an offering unto the Lord: whosoever is of a *willing heart*.**
> **Exodus 35:5**

The amount of that offering was so great, the Bible says it was *more than enough*. It was so much that the people had to be restrained from giving.

> **...The people bring *much more than enough* for the service of the work, which the Lord commanded to make.**
>
> **And Moses gave commandment...Let neither man nor woman make any more work for the offering of the sanctuary. So the people were *restrained from bringing*.**
> **Exodus 35:5,6**

If you put a limit on the amount you will give to God, you do not have a willing mind. In this state of mind, you will not be able to give the amount He wants you to give. Only when you are of a totally willing mind will you be able to give a proper offering without reservation.

> **For if there be first a willing mind...**
> **2 Corinthians 8:12**

Step Two: You must only think of the good things.

Most Christians make a terrible mistake when they are deciding how much to give in an offering. They allow their minds to be filled with the wrong things. Instead of concentrating on the things *they have*, their mind wanders to the things *they do not have*. For instance, they will begin to think about the new tires they *need* instead of concentrating on the automobile *God has given them.*

When your mind is fixed on your needs, there is a natural tendency to lower the amount of money you are *willing* to give God. You must fix your mind on the good things God has already provided for you. If you do this, you will have a tendency to give the amount God tells you.

That is why the Apostle Paul told the Corinthians to give according to what they *had* instead of according to what they *did not have.*

> **...it** (the offering) **is accepted according to that a man hath** (his blessings)**, and not according to that he hath not** (his shortage).
> **2 Corinthians 8:12**

It is reasonable to assume that if your mind is full of the blessings God has given you, your spirit will be much more open to His instructions as to how much to give. God wants you to give according to the good things He has given you, not according to the shortage Satan has caused in your life. Do not penalize God for the devil's work. Reward your God according to the blessings He has already brought you.

> **...it is accepted according to that a man hath.**
> **2 Corinthians 8:12**

Step Three: You must determine the amount you give will be given cheerfully.

The spirit in which a gift is given always has an effect on the person to whom the gift is given. Some people are able to make you feel bad, or even guilty, when they give to you. Some even give with a martyr's complex. They actually put on a long face and sad eyes as they tell you in great detail of the tremendous sacrifice they are making to give you the gift. They will let you know you must be very careful with what they give you, for they will suffer much for giving it to you.

God has no pleasure in an offering given in the wrong attitude. This is made clear in this scripture:

> **...cheerful givers are the ones God prizes.**
> **2 Corinthians 9:7** TLB

> **...God loveth a cheerful giver.**
> **2 Corinthians 9:7**

The Living Bible says God *prizes* cheerful givers. The *King James Version* says He *loves* cheerful givers. Both translations make it clear that He prefers receiving from those who give cheerfully.

Think how you would feel if a person who made you feel bad every time he gave you something asked you how much he should give you. Even if you did need something, your answer would probably be, "Oh, no. I don't want you to give me anything." You would answer this way to keep from having to feel bad after receiving from him.

I believe God has the same attitude toward grumpy givers. He will be reluctant to tell them how much to put in an offering.

If you want to enjoy the status of one of God's *preferred givers*, you must remain cheerful while giving. God is eager to reveal this exact amount He wants given if He is speaking to a cheerful giver.

> **...cheerful givers are the ones God prizes.**
> **2 Corinthians 9:7** TLB

Step Four: You must refuse to give when man puts pressure on you.

It is better to give nothing than to give an amount someone pressures you into. This does not mean that when people emphasize the urgency of the need, they are putting pressure on you to give. They may simply be relaying to you the pressure *they are under*.

If your pastor tells you of an emergency need, this should not be considered pressure. If he emphasizes that everyone will have to give a generous amount, he is simply giving you vital information about the *size of the need*.

Pressurized giving takes place when psychological force is used to cause you to give more than God is telling you to give. The Scriptures are clear on this matter. Do not feel guilty if you do not give when pressure is applied. The Bible places the responsibility on the one who is taking the offering not to apply pressure to the ones who are giving.

> *...Don't force anyone to give more than he really wants to* **for cheerful givers are the ones God prizes.**
> **2 Corinthians 9:7** TLB

If you feel that psychological pressure is being applied or the amount God says to give is not large enough, *do not give anything at that time.* God has said His people should never feel forced to give more than they really want to give. When you feel pressure, you can be sure the offering is not being taken properly.

Please note, this does not necessarily mean the offering is not being taken for a good purpose. It is proof that it is not being taken in a proper manner. The application of pressure does not mean God does not want you to give. It only means the one taking the offering is not familiar with God's due order, or he is not trusting God to speak to His children about the need. While the application of pressure does make an offering suspect, it does not disqualify it from being valid.

If pressure has been applied, my advice is to wait for a few days to pass. If you still feel a burden after this time, apply these six steps. God will reaffirm to you the amount He wants you to give.

Remember, it is the responsibility of the person taking the offering to take it properly.

> **...Don't force anyone to give more than he really wants to....**
>
> **2 Corinthians 9:7** TLB

Step Five: *You must let God impress you with a specific amount.*

Many people are confused by the term, "hearing from God," or "letting God speak to you." There are numerous ways God communicates with His children. The way I have found to be most common is by impression. In this method of communication, God will impress your consciousness with a certain amount of money He wants you to give. Keep in mind that this is not the only way God communicates with His children. It is the most common way.

When you are deciding how much you should give, several different amounts may come to your mind. We have all heard well-meaning ministers say if two amounts of money come to your mind, the larger amount is the one God wants you to give. They say the lower amount is the one the devil wants you to give. If you will just think about this, you will quickly realize the devil will *never* tell anyone to give *any amount* of money to God.

It is possible that neither of the two amounts that come to your mind are what God wants you to give. Then again, it might be the highest figure. It is even possible that it might be the lower figure. Here is a scripture that will always help you choose the amount God is telling you to give.

> **...let the peace of God *rule* in your hearts....**
>
> **Colossians 3:15**

The English word *rule* in this verse does not properly convey the full meaning of the Greek word that is used in the original text. The literal meaning of the word is better translated *umpire*. Paul said to let the *peace of God* be the *umpire* in our hearts. When you are faced with conflicting amounts of money to give, always give the amount you have God's peace with.

Let the presence of God's peace in your heart make the decision for you. Only when you have His perfect peace will you be able to give with confidence, knowing the amount of your offering is correct.

> ...let the peace of God *rule* in your hearts....
> **Colossians 3:15**

Step Six: *You must only give when you can believe God will give back to you.*

The Bible says if we do not act in faith, *it is sin.* I have never heard anyone say a person could give in such a way that it would be considered sin. However, the Bible says:

> ...Whatsoever is not of faith is sin.
> **Romans 14:23**

If you do not expect anything back from God when you give to Him, you *have not* given in faith. See the Bible's definition of faith.

> ...faith is the substance of things *hoped for.*
> **Hebrews 11:1**

God's Word says that whatever is given to Him will be given back to the giver.

> *Give*, **and** *it shall be given unto you;* **good measure, pressed down, and shaken together, and running over, shall men give into your bosom....**
> **Luke 6:38**

To give correctly, *you must have a desired return in mind.* If you are *not* hoping for something back from Him, you are not giving in faith.

From the Scriptures we can conclude that when God tells you how much to give, you *must* have the faith to believe He will give it back to you. If for some reason you have trouble believing God will multiply back to you that which you are about to give, don't despair. There is a prayer that will remove unbelief.

> *...help thou mine unbelief.*
>
> **Mark 9:24**

Give only when you have enough faith to believe God will give it back to you, for **...Whatsoever is not of faith is sin** (Rom. 14:23).

Let's review the six steps to follow to know how much money to give in an offering:

Step One: You must have a willing mind.

Step Two: You must only think of the good things.

Step Three: You must determine the amount you give will be given cheerfully.

Step Four: You must refuse to give when man puts pressure on you.

Step Five: You must let God impress you with a specific amount.

Step Six: You must only give when you can believe God will give back to you.

Begin today. Put these six steps to work in determining how much your offerings should be. You will be surprised how much difference it will make in the way God is able to bless you.

I suggest that you jot down these six steps in the front of your Bible. Experience has proven that if you use these six steps, you will never have to feel that you have missed God in an offering. Try it. You will like the result it brings.

6

His Abundance,
Your Responsibility

Galatians 6:6-9 best begins to clarify the concepts that have been covered so far, and serves to summarize the substance of the giving spirit:

> **Let him that is taught in the word communicate unto** (share with) **him that teacheth in all good things.**
>
> **Be not deceived; God is not mocked: for whatsoever a man soweth, that shall he also reap.**
>
> **For he that soweth to his flesh shall of the flesh reap corruption; but he that soweth to the Spirit shall of the Spirit reap life everlasting.**
>
> **And let us not be weary in well doing: for in due season we shall reap, if we faint not.**

In verse 6 God says to share your good things with your teachers. These are not my words; God says it! You have a responsibility to share with your local church, Christian television, a book or tape ministry — wherever your teachers are, the Word says to share your good things with them.

God wants you to act first — to sow the seed, so you can begin to reap. This is clearly seen in verses 7 and 8. God will not be mocked.

In verse 9, God answers the question people often ask: "Brother John, I gave $25 to the Lord two weeks ago, and I haven't received anything back."

God's reply? **Let us not be weary in well doing: for in due season we shall reap, if we faint not.**

What farmer would plant a seed in the ground and expect to see a plant the next day? What farmer would plant a seed one day, then dig it up the next to see how it was growing?

Please begin to grasp the total giving plan as God has worked it out for your life:

1. You must act first. God will respond when you plant the first seed.

2. When you plant your seed, you free Him to bless your life with harvest.

3. The harvest is always abundant, but in relation to the amount of seed planted. Plant a little, and God will return the seed multiplied. Plant a lot, and God will return a lot — multiplied.

4. It is not enough that you simply give; you must give for His purposes, for His work, where His meat is being given to His people.

5. As He returns your gifts *back* to you, increased, you have the responsibility to turn right around and plant some more seed for *His* purposes. As you show you are trustworthy of His gifts, His blessings for your life will increase.

The salvation of the world depends upon Christians like you fully grasping and applying these principles in their walk with the Lord. The *informed* child of God knows that God wants us to give so He can give back to us, so we can give again to His purposes! God wants us to give, not just so we can benefit, but also for the benefit of lost souls needing to hear His message.

People on the next block, people in Africa, people in Atlanta, people in China — people everywhere are waiting to hear the Gospel.

But let's not fool ourselves. These people will not just wake up one day and realize they need Jesus. They need someone to tell them, and it takes money to send the literature and the preachers to those places.

Romans 10:14,15 makes some very specific points about this problem.

How then shall they call on him in whom they have not believed? and how shall they believe in him of whom they have not heard? and how shall they hear without a preacher?

And how shall they preach, except they be sent?

Every single person who ever received salvation was told about Jesus by someone; someone delivered the Word, and someone gave to send that preacher.

Praise God! He has the total power of the universe; He has more than enough! But God has voluntarily limited Himself. He cannot, He will not, release His wealth, His riches, His abundance until *somebody* puts to work His laws of *giving to receive!*

You may be saying: "Oh, that man! He is just trying to get me to give some money to his ministry." No, that is not what I am trying to do. I am trying to get you to pay attention to what God says.

The Word says to tithe to the ministry that is your storehouse, that provides you with meat. Give to any ministry that nourishes you with the Word of God. If *my* ministry provides you with the Word of God, then by all means give not to us, but to *God's work* going on through us.

If you do not like what I am saying here, if you do not care for how all of this sounds, you have no argument with me. Your argument is with the *Word of God*.

Yes, you need to give your money to this ministry, or to any other ministry that preaches the Word of God. You need to give where you are nourished in order that souls will be saved, and in order that you might receive more back from God, so you can give again and again, each time more abundantly — for His purposes.

The unsaved world is just sitting there waiting for the saints, the children of God, to put this principle to work in their lives.

Don't keep them waiting for eternity. Plant your seed for their souls today.

7

In You God Trusts

When we studied God's law concerning giving in the earlier chapters, we discovered some shocking truths. We discovered something exactly opposite from that which is often taught: expecting to receive is a godly way to give.

If that blew your mind, then hold onto your hat for this next truth, because it shocks everyone who hears it for the first time. In Luke 16:11 it says:

> **If therefore ye have not been faithful in the unrighteous mammon, who will commit to your trust the true riches?**

Once again, we see God's ways are not the ways of man. It seems only natural that if you were faithful in spiritual matters, then God would trust you with money and wealth. But that is not what the verse says.

The verse clearly states that we must be *first* faithful in money matters, and then God will trust us with "true riches" — the spiritual and eternal matters.

The motto on our coins and money in the United States is *"In God We Trust."* Have you ever thought that the reverse is *also* true? *In You God Trusts.*

This is backwards to the way most Christians were taught to think. This is a truth that you must begin to absorb, however, if you truly desire spiritual responsibility in your life. You must first be faithful with your money before God will trust you with spiritual matters.

Oh, I can hear some of you saying as you read this: "Brother John, don't tell me that stuff about my finances. I am trying so hard to be faithful to God, but I just do not have much money."

Do not let the devil lie to you about this matter. You will never be strong with God if you are not faithful to God in your finances. Read Luke 16:11 again:

> **If therefore ye have not been faithful in the unrighteous mammon, who will commit to your trust the true riches?**

These are not *my* words; they are God's. This is not *my* law; it is God's. This is not *my* principle; it is God's.

Let me refer you to a beautiful illustration of God's principle in Second Kings. The house of God was in need of repair. Whom did the king call upon to repair it? He chose men who could be trusted with money. He picked the carpenters, the brick masons, based on their *past record* of faithfulness.

When King Josiah was told to build the Lord's house, he called together the carpenters, masons, and hewers of wood and stone, and in Second Kings 22:7 he states:

> **Howbeit there was no reckoning made with them of the money that was delivered into their hand, because they dealt faithfully.**

Dear reader, it is important that the king used the past tense, *dealt*. These men were not chosen because they promised to deal faithfully with money, or because it appeared that if they were given money, they could handle it. No, they were chosen because they had already *proven* they could handle their financial affairs; they had already *dealt* with the financial area of their lives.

These workers had been working on all types of secular ventures. They had learned their trades in other building projects, but had always been faithful in their financial matters. So when it came time for the king to choose who would do the work on the house of God, God told the king to choose men who had dealt properly with their finances.

But you say: "Brother John, can my finances really be that important to God?"

Is His Word *that* important to you?

Over and over, the Bible deals with money and how God expects us to handle our finances — how we are supposed to operate with our financial responsibilities. If it is important to God, shouldn't it be important to you?

These builders were so faithful in their finances that they did not even have a "reckoning made"; no receipts were demanded for their expenditures!

The tradesmen were chosen not because they were *going* to deal faithfully, but because they *had dealt* faithfully with their finances. The carpenters were those carpenters who had given a part of their income for the things of God. The masons were those who had been proper in their finances.

Read again those words of Luke 16:11:

> If therefore ye have not been faithful in the unrighteous mammon, who will commit to your trust the true riches?

In you God trusts. God uses people who are faithful in their finances. These are the ones who receive the true treasures, the true spiritual responsibilities.

First, be faithful with your money; then the true riches of God shall be given unto you.

The next verse in Luke has equal shock value for the Christian who is reading with an open mind, and the blessing of the Spirit:

> **And if ye have not been faithful in that which is another man's, who shall give you that which is your own?**

Some people have asked me, "Brother John, I feel the Lord is leading me to start a ministry, but the finances just are not there yet; what should I do?"

My answer? Read Luke 16:12.

Faithfulness to the ministry of another is the prerequisite to your having a ministry of your own. That scripture clearly shows that if you do not faithfully support the ministry of someone else, then you will never have one of your own.

This verse shocks the senses of the average Christian, but it is the logical extension of the law of sowing and reaping. How can you plant your own ministry without first planting ministry seeds somewhere else? People can run all over the world trying to get their ministries started, but the key to God's spiritual success is clear:

> **And if ye have not been faithful in that which is another man's, who shall give you that which is your own?**

As you are faithful to God in your finances, He has a very special reward for you. It is not a crown. It is not the honor of sitting in a certain place in heaven. It is not a hilltop mansion on Hallelujah Boulevard.

But His reward is so special that any person committed to God would hunger to receive it.

This special reward is found in Matthew 25:15-23 which deals with the servant and the talents.

One servant had five talents, another had two talents, and another had one talent entrusted to his care. When the master left, the servant with five talents increased them to ten. He doubled what he had and was a good steward before the Lord. The one with two talents used them properly and returned four to his Lord. But the one with a single talent buried it in the ground. He did nothing with it.

Who received rewards? The two servants who had increased their talents. Listen to what the Word of God says they were to receive for their reward:

Well done, thou good and faithful servant: thou hast been faithful over a few things, I will make thee ruler over many things.

Wouldn't that be the greatest reward of all — to be able to hear Jesus Christ say to you: "Well done, thou good and faithful servant?"

No mansion could compete with that glory! No place on Hallelujah Boulevard would be so sweet. No crown would wear quite as well as those words. Oh, the feeling of joy that would come, for the Lord to look over and say: "Come here, thou good and faithful servant."

That reward is yours in eternity, but it must be purchased here. You must take whatever God gives you — one talent, two talents, and plant it in his work, so He can multiply it again to be used for His glory, the plan of salvation. It is the only way I know of whereby God can say to you: "Well done, my good and faithful servant."

And notice the other key line in this passage: "Thou hast been faithful over a few things (maybe you only have little money); I will make thee ruler over many things."

If you want to rule over many things, if you want God to trust you with the true riches, if you expect God to honor your own ministry, then your path is clear. Hear His Word and obey it.

8

Faithfulness —
The Divine Expectation

It seems as though the children of God go through many different phases in their Christian walks. One of the popular cries I often hear is: "Oh, I just know the Lord is getting ready to use me in a *mighty way.*"

Maybe He is getting ready to use you in a mighty way, but it is my experience that He expects some basic things from us first, and the most essential expectation is our *faithfulness* to Him.

I do not think there is anything nearer to God's heart than faithful stewards who work and accomplish His purpose each and every day. In the last chapter, we saw the reward for the faithful servant. In this one, let us look a bit deeper into the area of faithfulness.

Let me show you a verse of scripture with such a powerful thought to it that I want you to let it infiltrate your life; memorize it, and then practice it diligently as part of your daily relationship with God. The scripture is First Corinthians 4:2, which reads: **Moreover it is required in stewards, that a man be found faithful.**

Notice it says not *mighty*, but *faithful*.

And notice, please, it doesn't say it is desired, or it is suggested, or it would be nice if, it says *it is required.*

There is a great deal of difference between that which is desired and that which is required. There are many desirable things a steward could have: talent, natural ability, good personality, and energy. But none of those qualities will fulfill the Biblical requirement for stewardship: *faithfulness.*

There are many ways the Lord can use your life for Him, but if you want to be a good steward, it is required that you be faithful.

He tells us that if we are going to be counted upon as stewards in the house of God and attend to the important matters of His Father's house, we will have to be faithful.

There are four main areas in which I believe God's stewards must be faithful:

1. *Faithful in prayer.*

Pray for all of these vehicles now functioning to bring about His endtime plan: your local church body, the missionaries going to foreign lands, and the radio and television ministries reaching the shut-ins and the unchurched. All of these properties of God need your constant, unceasing prayer so God's will for this planet will be accomplished.

2. *Faithful in witnessing.*

God wants you to be not only a praying Christian; He wants you to be a *speaking* Christian.

All four Gospels end with he same exhortation as that of Luke 24:47,48:

> **And that repentance and remission of sins should be preached in his name among all nations, beginning at Jerusalem.**

And ye are *witnesses* of these things.

God wants you to share His forgiveness and love in all corners of the world, beginning at Jerusalem; that is, beginning in your own neighborhood.

Galilee was Christ's own backyard, and He preached and performed miracles there *first*, before He went, or would let His apostles go any other place.

So, too, with you! Many of you feel a calling to go off into a foreign field to preach His Word. Many of you feel God calling you to another place.

Before you go, ask yourself if you are being a good steward where you are. Are you leaving your Jerusalem before you have functioned there as a faithful steward?

3. *Faithful in living.*

The only Gospel many people will ever know, the only Gospel they will ever come in touch with, is your life as you live the Christian way before them. At work by the water cooler, you are either reflecting His glory or you are speaking in a way that reflects the world.

The world has so many mammoth problems. Often people come to me and ask questions like:

"Brother John, what can I possibly do to prevent nuclear war?"

"Not much," I tell them, "but through the power of Christ in you, you can do anything. You can pray against nuclear war, and God will honor your prayer."

Be faithful in your praying. Be faithful in your witnessing, and be faithful in living your Christian life. **Be ye doers of the word, and not hearers only** (James 1:22).

4. *Faithful in giving.*

We have seen earlier in this book what a joy it is to give to the Lord. We have seen that when we give with the right heart, to help further His will on earth, He returns to us our gift in abundance so we can give again for His glory.

The Lord takes the financial responsibilities of stewardship very seriously. We saw in Galatians 6:7:

> **Be not deceived; God is not mocked; for whatsoever a man soweth, that shall he also reap.**

Now turn to Ecclesiastes 5:4,5 to understand what God expects when we pledge our finances for His glory:

> **When thou vowest a vow unto God, defer not to pay it; for he hath no pleasure in fools: pay that which thou hast vowed.**
>
> **Better is it that thou shouldest not vow, than that thou shouldest vow and not pay.**

I believe and know that you no longer need to be fed only spiritual milk; you are ready for meat. Praise God!

Preachers have been telling us lately how much God loves us, and He does; and how much God wants to have a personal relationship with us, and He does — but some of them forget to remind you that God has divine expectations for us — and believe me, He does.

He has given us life, expecting to receive back from us service, love, obedience, worship, praise, and fellowship.

He has given us our finances, expecting to receive some of it back for His plan.

I know that as the Spirit deals with you as you read this book, your life will fall into complete order and stewardship for His glory in all areas of your life: praying, witnessing, living, and giving.

9

Your Eye in the Sky

When I was a young boy, I would often indulge in a particular fantasy as I played in my own private world. In this fantasy I imagined an all-seeing, gigantic eye that would always watch out for me. If someone tried to beat me up, the eye would save me. If I was having problems in school, the eye would come to my aid. I imagined this powerful, all-seeing eye knew all about me, watched over me, and met every need in my life.

Naturally, these fantasies took place *before* I was saved. After Christ became a reality in my life, I realized the "eye" I had only imagined was indeed a living reality in the person of my faithful God.

God is continuously watching out for you and me. He is your eye in the sky. God doesn't want harm or danger or enemies or misfortune to rule your life. God promises He will be the source of your protection, the watchful eye your life. But, as you learned in an earlier chapter of this book, all of God's promises have conditions. In Psalm 101:6, we read:

> **Mine eyes shall be upon the faithful of the land, that they may dwell with me: he that walketh in a perfect way, he shall serve me.**

In a previous chapter we learned that God has a strict requirement for the life of a steward — faithfulness. Now we see God has a promise for His faithful stewards:

Mine eyes shall be upon the faithful of the land, that they may dwell with me.

God's condition is *if* you are a faithful steward. God's promise is that His eyes shall be upon the faithful *and* that they may dwell with Him. Wouldn't you like to be counted among those who have *His eye*, who are able to dwell with Him? His promise is conditional upon your faithfulness.

In this day and age it seems there are so many terrible things going on in the world. The horrible sin of murder is being disguised in the clinical-sounding name of "abortion." Rape victims suffer, while rapists roam the streets free when courts bend in ridiculous attempts to grant the criminal "his rights."

Young thugs think nothing of knocking down an old lady to steal a few dollars from her purse. Financial problems are rampant in middle-class America, and bankruptcy proceedings are now commonplace and accepted.

In the midst of this, wouldn't it be wonderful to know that God's eyes are continuously upon you? Wouldn't it be a comfort to know that God knows about the next house payment you have to make, the next bill you have to pay, the next item of clothing you have to buy — and to know that He cares about it, and that He will help you to do something to meet those financial obligations?

He promises that kind of involvement to you if you are faithful to Him. He does not get involved on a day-to-day basis with those who are not faithful to Him. The Bible clearly says, **Without faith, it is impossible**

to please him (God) (Heb. 11:6). But read what He says will happen to the faithful in Psalm 31:23,24:

> **O love the Lord, all ye his saints: for the Lord preserveth the faithful, and plentifully rewardeth the proud doer.**
>
> **Be of good courage, and he shall strengthen your heart, all ye that hope in the Lord.**

God watches over the faithful and plentifully rewards the proud doer! God watches over you *if* you are *faithful* to Him.

If you are faithful to God, He will be just like that eye I imagined as a child. He will be looking over your shoulder; He will see those bills that need to be paid and that problem with your family that needs special attention, and He will *faithfully* deal with it.

It is a frightful thing to live in a world where inflation runs unchecked. Interest rates could double what they were only a few years ago. Gasoline prices could double or even triple as they have in the past. A simple automobile today costs more than a complete home did when I was a boy.

Yet, with your God watching, with His eye upon you, you can be at peace. You can go to bed tonight knowing that every need you have is being met by your God. As long as you are faithful to Him, He knows about the bill sitting on your desk that must be paid tomorrow and He knows the way for you to pay it!

Let me encourage you not to despair over the circumstances of your life, but rather, to lift your head and rejoice. Know that if you are faithful, God will take care of all of your needs.

Some of you reading this are skeptical. You are saying: "Well, Brother John, this all sounds real nice, but it still seems like you are engaging in adult fantasy. Life simply does not work in the way you describe it here, with God looking out for my every need."

Read carefully First Thessalonians 5:24: **Faithful is he that calleth you, who also will do it**. Those are precious words. **Faithful is he that calleth you.** I like that.

Right now, you may really need to read and understand the spirit of those words. He is faithful to you, and will do it. He will do what needs to be done in your life.

Whatever your problem, God will deal with it; He will do it, for He is faithful. You simply cannot believe one part of the Word and reject another. Either it is all true, or none of it is true. There can be no compromise.

Why is it so easy for us as Christians to believe God will judge unbelievers, but so hard for us to believe God will reward those who are righteous? Look what Jesus said: **I will never leave you nor forsake you** (Heb. 13:5).

Burn that into your mind, into your spirit. Let Satan's lie that "God does not care about you" die once and for all.

God is faithful to us — that is His promise to those who are faithful to Him.

What did David say in Psalm 37:25? How magnificently he put it!

> **I have been young, and now am old; yet have I not seen the righteous forsaken, nor his seed begging bread.**

Glory be to God! We serve a God who is faithful.

The next passage I want you to read here is a little long, but I want to quote it all to you because it is essential that this become part of your very being. Look at Matthew 6:25-33:

> Therefore, I say unto you, Take no thought for your life, what ye shall eat, or what ye shall drink; nor yet for your body, what ye shall put on. Is not the life more than meat, and the body than raiment?
>
> Behold the fowls of the air: for they sow not, neither do they reap, nor gather into barns; yet your heavenly Father feedeth them. Are ye not much better than they?
>
> Which of you by taking thought can add one cubit unto his stature?
>
> And why take ye thought for raiment? Consider the lilies of the field, how they grow; they toil not, neither do they spin:
>
> And yet I say unto you, That even Solomon in all his glory was not arrayed like one of these.
>
> Wherefore, if God so clothe the grass of the field, which to day is, and to morrow is cast into the oven, shall he not much more clothe you, O ye of little faith?
>
> Therefore take no thought, saying, What shall we eat? or, What shall we drink? or, Wherewithal shall we be clothed?
>
> (For after all these things do the Gentiles seek:) for your heavenly Father knoweth that ye have need of all these things.
>
> But seek ye first the kingdom of God, and his righteousness; and all these things shall be added unto you.

In this precious passage, we are told not to worry about what we are going to eat or drink or wear. Let's face it; in today's world, when you talk about food and clothing, you are talking about the greater part of your expenses in this life. Our God says He knows of these needs in your life, and will supply them. This passage in paraphrase simply says:

> Beloved, look out your window, and see how faithful I am. You see that bird over there? He doesn't sow, he doesn't reap, he doesn't have a job or a lunch bucket or a credit card. But every day and every minute I take care of the little fellow. He can't even fall to the ground without My knowing about it.

Perhaps the most beautiful and comforting line in the Scriptures ends the passage:

> **. . . for your heavenly Father knoweth that ye have need of all these things.**

> **But seek ye first the kingdom of God, and his righteousness; and all these things shall be added unto you.**

His promise? Be faithful, and I will take care of you. God will be faithful to you. He wants you always abounding in the good things of the Lord.

As you sow *faithfulness* to Him, you will reap a harvest of His abundant faithfulness back to you!

10

Who Signs Your Paycheck?

In a previous chapter, we saw that God will honor your faithfulness, that He will take care of those who abide in His will. I hope your spirit is now beginning to grasp that as you are faithful to God, He will in return be faithful to you in all of your needs.

In Second Corinthians 1:20, there is a scripture that perfectly describes God's attitude toward His promises:

> **For all the promises of God in him are yea, and in him Amen, unto the glory of God by us.**

God tells you, that all of His promises are yes — so be it. Everything that God has promised for your life, He will deliver to you. If you fail to get anything else out of this book, understand this: God and His promises are *your source*.

You may be thinking: "Why, Brother John, that all *sounds nice*, but *my job* is my source — it's what pays all of my bills."

No, you are wrong! God is your source. Your job is just the current circumstance God uses to bless you. But your boss does not sign your paycheck; God does! His name may not be on it, but if you are a faithful steward, I guarantee you — and the Word guarantees you — His blessings are in it, just as though God himself had signed that check on payday.

Your boss and your employer are not your source. Now, you may have a very fine employer and you may work for a very good boss, but all of that is nothing more than the instrument that God, your source, uses to get to you the wealth He wants you to have.

Your talent is not your source. Right now, God may be using you as a carpenter, or an electrician, or a secretary, or a computer expert. But make no mistake about it, God can use you for His glory no matter what your talent. If you are open and faithful to Him, then He will bless you, no matter what your particular talent is.

No company, no talent, no boss, no political party, no worker's union — none of these is your source. The only true source you have is your great God, and He is all you need!

All of the circumstances and talents in your life are only the instruments that God can use to bless you. God could get His wealth to you even if you did not have a job. God has the ability to take care of His children.

In every country I go into, I find God's people are prospering. God is getting His wealth and prosperity to His people throughout the world, no matter where they live.

Your job is not your source. Right now, you may be in real estate — and the circumstances may say the housing market is moving very slowly. Yet, every day some piece of property is being sold. God can bring you a buyer if you only trust Him and are faithful to His expectations. If you look to God, He will meet all of your needs.

In Second Peter 1:3, we see how totally God wants to involve Himself in our lives.

> **According as his divine power hath given us all things that pertain unto life and godliness, through the knowledge of him that hath called us to glory and virtue....**

It is His divine will to give us all things that pertain to life and godliness.

I'm excited to be able to tell you that God does sign your paycheck! I'm excited to tell you that no matter what the current economic circumstances indicate, no matter what E. F. Hutton says, no matter what the state of the country looks like, God can provide.

You have His Word on it.

You may be shaking your head, saying: "Well then, Brother John, if God signs my paycheck, then when is He going to give me a promotion?"

I'm happy to say the Bible answers that question, too. Turn to Psalm 75:6,7:

> **For promotion cometh neither from the east, nor from the west, nor from the south.**
>
> **But God is the judge: he putteth down one, and setteth up another.**

Look to God for your promotion. Psalm 75 says He is in charge of promotion matters.

You do not have to look to your superintendent or to your boss; if you are looking to God as your source, He gives the promotion.

Notice in the passage that the directions covered are east, west, and south. What happened to north?

Promotion *does come* from the north. The throne of God is in the north.

As a child of God, learn that your promotion on your job will come if you go to God, expecting Him to do the arbitration for you, expecting God to burden the hearts of those around you to give you the promotion.

As with any promise from God, there are things you must do. If you are a slothful saint, do not expect just to lie back and let God give you a promotion. God is not in favor of slothfulness and will not reward it.

But if you are working properly and are an honest, hard worker, then go to God and ask Him to begin the arbitration process. Continue to put the interests of the company you work for ahead of your own, and God guarantees He will protect and watch out for your interests.

God is able to promote you. And the best part about His ability is that when God decides one of His children is to be promoted, then no person on this earth can cheat him or her out of it.

How many times have I heard someone say: "Oh, I was about to get a promotion, but then the relative of the boss came in and cheated me out of it."

When the God of heaven decides it is time for you to be promoted, then no relative, no boss, no circumstance can stop the process.

Getting a promotion on your job is a very simple process:

1. Become a good worker, an honest worker, giving your employer a full measure of energy for the time you are on the job.

2. Live your life as a good steward, in accordance with the will of God.

3. Use your time wisely on the job, and work for the interests of your company, turning your own interests over to the protection and intercession of the Father.

4. Express to God in prayer your desire for promotion, and tell Him you know He is your source, your boss, and the one who is in charge of your promotion.

"But Brother John, you don't know my boss. He just doesn't seem to like me. He has it in for me."

God is in charge, and He can change hearts. In Proverbs 21:1, the Word says:

> **The king's heart is in the hand of the Lord, as the rivers of water: he turneth it withersoever he will.**

God can change the heart of a king, and He can change your boss' mind, your superintendent's mind, your company's mind.

God not only signs your paycheck, He is in charge of your promotion!

11

Wealth, Profit, and the Prophets

By now you are well aware that this is not the usual Christian book. We have explored some shocking and tradition-shattering ideas about giving, receiving, and money. In this chapter, the shock of God's Word will continue to shake your spirit, and help you break out of the shackles of financial bondage that some of Satan's lies may have put you in.

In the last chapter, we said God is the source of all of your needs; He signs your paycheck and gives you your promotion. Now I want you to know that *God is the power that allows you to receive wealth!*

At that point, Brother Skeptic may have fallen out of his chair. "Now hold on there, Brother John," He is shouting. "Enough is enough." Well, Skeptic, sit back down on your chair and read Deuteronomy 8:18 with me:

> But thou shalt remember the Lord thy God: for it is he that giveth thee power to get wealth, that he may establish his covenant which he sware unto thy fathers, as it is this day.

Once again we have a controversial idea — God gives you the power to obtain wealth. The idea is not mine! If you have any problems with this concept, please take them up with the author of Deuteronomy.

The Bible says God is the One who gives you the power to get wealth. Any skill, trade, profession, vocation — anything that helps you earn income — that ability comes from God.

So often we are taught that when we have a spiritual problem, we go to the Lord. But He cares not only about your spirit; He cares about *all* of you.

If you have a desire to increase your capacity to earn income, then seek out the Lord. Ask Him where you should go to improve your skills. If you go to the Lord and seek answers for your financial situation, He wants to help. What better employment counselor could you have than the great God of heaven?

> ...it is he that giveth thee power to get wealth....

In the natural, that sounds almost like a vulgar and crass concept. In the spiritual, when you see your Father as someone who cares about all aspects of your life — even the financial — it becomes just another tribute to the giving, loving, concerned nature of our Creator.

One of the names given to Him in the Bible is the *Mighty God, Counselor*. So you really think that God would ask you to give something — tithes and offerings — to Him, that He did not give you the ability to get? Of course not.

Do you think God would put it on your heart to give a hundred or a thousand dollars to a gospel project, and then not give you the means to honor that pledge? Of course not.

I believe God does burden your heart to give to a certain project, and I believe God does provide you with the ability to honor that pledge. Whenever I am in a crusade or any place where there is a challenge to reach lost souls, I want to get involved with the money God has entrusted to my stewardship. God has never let me down; each time I make a pledge for His work, He gives me the ability to meet that pledge.

Why?

> **But thou shalt remember the Lord thy God: for it is He that giveth thee power to get wealth, that he may establish his covenant which he sware unto thy fathers, as it is this day.**
>
> **Deuteronomy 8:18**

The Lord not only directs what you are to give, but He also provides you the ability to receive. He has in His hand, and in His power, the ability to prosper you, to speak to you and guide you as you become more and more obedient to His will.

When God gives you a burden to do something, the very God of heaven can also bring it to pass, because it is He who gives you the power to get wealth. The skill is in your hands; the ability is in your mind. The power is from God.

The special talent you have, whatever it is, has been given to you by God — and the proceeds from some of that talent should be used to further the Kingdom of God here on earth.

As God is the source of your paycheck, of your promotion, and even of your wealth, He is also the source of your profit! In Isaiah 48:17,18, we read:

> **Thus saith the Lord, thy Redeemer, the Holy One of Israel; I am the Lord thy God which teacheth thee to profit, which leadeth thee by the way that thou shouldest go.**

> O that thou hadst hearkened to my command-
> ments! then had thy peace been as a river, and thy
> righteousness as the waves of the sea.

This scripture is especially important for those of
you who are in charge of your own companies, your
own businesses. Here is a case where a prophet can
teach you how to profit!

The Word of God says:

> I am the Lord thy God which teacheth thee to
> profit. . . .

This verse speaks especially to the businessman
in today's society. Note it talks *only* to the Christian
businessman; it reads, "thy Redeemer," so it applies
to a special person: the Christian business person.

From this verse it is evident that God wants to
become *your* partner — He wants to teach you how to
profit. Any full- or part-time business demands special
skills. You do not go out and buy a fruit stand, a meat
market, or a computer store and simply start your
business. You must have skill. You need to know about
fruit if you are going to sell fruit. You need to know
the difference between shank and loin if you are selling
meat. You need to know the definition of C.P.U. and
why it is important, if you are selling computers.

You must have a skill. But, just as important, you
need to have proper timing. You have often heard it
said: "He was in the right place at the right time."

Well, who is better to look to for guidance about
where to be and when to be there, than your God? Look
at that scripture again. He says, **I am the Lord thy God
which teacheth thee to profit** and **which leadeth thee
by the way that thou shouldest go**.

God is telling you He will lead you in the way you should go. As you let the Lord start to lead you, you will find yourself showing up at a certain place, wondering: "Why am I here today?" And as you are wondering, someone will come up to sit next to you, and an important business transaction will take place.

This is not fantasy. It says in His Word that He wants to lead you. I personally know businessmen who practice letting God lead them, and this very kind of thing often happens. Businessmen come up to me and say: "Brother John, I don't know why I was there that particular day, but I was, and the Lord brought into the same room just the person I needed to see — and in a matter of minutes, we completed a large business transaction."

God wants to lead you; let go and let Him. In prayer, ask Him were He wants you to go today, then listen for His guidance. Who knows better than God where to lead you to accomplish your task?

Let God be a partner in your business. In today's society, *stress* seems to be the occupational hazard of so many business people. There are management seminars in "How To Deal With Stress." Inventors have created special isolation booths where people float in the dark on a buoyant solution, allowing their stress to ease. Psychologists are highly paid to hear the haggard business person pour out one problem after another.

Praise Him that you do not need to attend stress seminars, to learn how to float, or to find a good psychologist! Read Isaiah 48:18:

**O that thou hadst hearkened to my command-
ments! then had thy peace been as a river, and thy
righteousness as the waves of the sea.**

God will show you how to profit. God will guide
you. But listen to this great promise He made: He says
He will lead you in the way of peace. He will give you
peace like a river.

In Hebrew, the word for peace is *shalom*. It means
well being, health, prosperity. God wants to teach you
how to be healthy and how to prosper in your business.
As you stay in His will and hearken to His
commandments, He will be the best partner your
business ever had.

Any business partner enters into a contract with
his other partner so that there are clear understandings
about the rewards of their mutual work. So it is with
God. He expects, as part of His partnership with you,
that you are first faithful to His commandments. You
cannot operate your business with lies, cheating, and
deception and then expect God to guide you. He will
not cooperate in ungodly endeavors.

So first keep His commandments, then allow Him
to guide you. As your business prospers, and you
receive profits, then the next obligation you have to your
partner is to reward Him for His work to give Him a
share of the gain. As you make profits with God in your
business, you need to give back some of those profits
to Him, for the things of God.

Right now, today, let God become your official
business partner. Let God begin to teach you how to
profit, how to be at the right place at the right time.
Let God share His *shalom*, His peace with you, bringing

your business the health, the prosperity, the peaceful-ness it needs. You will be blessed with God as your partner. And as He blesses you, be sure you return the blessing by giving part of His profit back into the things of God.

Dedicate your vocation, your business, to God.

Often, in our spiritual growth, we dedicate our lives to the Lord — our homes to the Lord — our children to the Lord. Today I would like each of you to dedicate your vocation, your job, your business, to the Lord.

If you are a bricklayer, then say: "Lord, you are in the bricklaying business now, right alongside of me. Please guide me and teach me."

If you are a computer analyst, then say: "Lord, you are now in the business of interpreting data, right alongside me. Please help me see what you want me to see, and know what you would have me know about these numbers and statistics."

There is a beautiful illustration of how God can elevate your job, your position, as He becomes a part of your daily life.

Early in the book of Exodus we find that the Lord is preparing something big for the life of Moses. Moses has been a wealthy young man, living for a long period of time in Pharaoh's house.

But in the third chapter of Exodus, Moses is living in the house of his father-in-law, Jethro, and his new job — his vocation — is shepherd, watching sheep on the backside of the desert. It is as a shepherd that

Moses meets God through the burning bush, in circumstances so sacred he is warned:

> **Draw not near here: put off thy shoes from off thy feet, for the place whereon thou standest is holy ground.**
>
> **Exodus 3:5**

When God begins to give Moses His plan, and tells Moses he will lead the children of Israel out of Egypt, Moses reacts as an earthly shepherd would:

> **And Moses said unto God, Who am I, that I should go unto Pharaoh, and that I should bring forth the children of Israel out of Egypt?**
>
> **Exodus 3:11**

You know, Moses was right! By himself he could do nothing; he was a simple shepherd, and had no particular power even over sheep, let alone over their entire land of Egypt! But see what God does.

God demands that Moses give to Him his staff — the symbol, the representation of his job as a shepherd. God takes this staff and performs miracles with it, then returns it to Moses.

> **And thou shalt take this rod in thine hand, wherewith thou shalt do signs.**
>
> **Exodus 4:17**

Look closely at what happens here:

1. Moses, a mere shepherd, encounters God.

2. Moses, in a humble statement of his own weakness, turns over to the Lord his profession, his shepherding, in the form of a staff.

3. The Lord blesses the staff, and now is in partnership with Moses, as He returns the staff.

4. Moses leaves the mountain still a shepherd, but with the extra dimension of now functioning with the blessing of God.

In chapter 4, verse 20, we see how this changes Moses' life:

> **And Moses took his wife and his sons, and set them upon an ass, and he returned to the land of Egypt: and Moses took the rod of God in his hand.**

Notice now that the rod, the symbol of his vocation, is no longer just a shepherd's rod, but it is the *rod of God*.

So, too, in your life. As you pray the words that give your job to the Lord, you make Him a partner, and then you can draw from His ability, His strength, and His advice.

Heed me, as this is one of the most important things you can ever absorb into your spirit. No matter how bad inflation gets, no matter how many people are out of work, no matter what the interest rates do, you can be secure in your job, in your finances, as you dedicate that responsibility, that function you perform, to God.

Like Moses, without God as your source you can only ask, ". . .Who am I?" But with God as part of your profession, your business, your vocation, then you have the power of God inside you — the same power that God gave Moses to lead an entire nation of people out of Egypt.

As you make your job a joint responsibility between you and God, so, too, He will help you in your giving — telling you where to give, helping you tithe, and seeing to it that you fulfill your responsibility to His ministry throughout the world.

12
Plant Your Seeds — To Harvest

So often in this book you have seen that the Lord's philosophy, the Lord's method of operating, is precisely the opposite of the world's materialistic thought. The Biblical laws of sowing shatter many traditional thoughts of this earth and often send even faithful Christians back to their Bibles in panic, anxiously turning pages. Like the Skeptic, they pray: "Lord, say it isn't so. That means I will have to change my mind, to readjust my way of thinking!" In the realm of the spirit, the Bible truth can often be painful.

But praise God, through His grace, and through His guidance, all things can be overcome! If you have made it this far in the book, then I believe you are ready to shatter some more of those old, traditional teachings.

In an earlier chapter, I touched upon the world philosophy about money. The world teaches:

1. Get all you can.

2. Can all you get.

3. Guard the can.

Economists everywhere encourage their investors to grab up every piece of property, buy up all the gold and silver, get the greater percentage of a corporation's stock...get all you can, and then hold it. These investment "portfolios" are a supposed source of security in these troubled times.

But look what is happening, even in the natural realm. Property taxes and housing values have slowed from their previous fast pace. Gold prices have dropped in the last few years, and silver investments were rocked over the hoarding by a few investors that caused value to drop drastically. Stock prices have been so up and down the past decade that many investors must be dizzy from the roller coaster ride.

The ways of the world simply are not working.

Well, then, what is God's philosophy? To answer that question look at Proverbs 11:24,25:

> **There is that scattereth, and yet increaseth; and there is that withholdeth more than is meat** (fitting), **but it tendeth to poverty.**
>
> **The liberal soul shall be made fat: and he that watereth shall be watered also himself.**

The Word is talking here about a person who scatters what he has all around, and still finds himself gaining *an increase*. This is not what the world teaches!

And look further. The Word says that as you withhold — as you keep your money put away in a safe place — this tends to produce poverty.

How prophetic those words have become. The safest place to put money when I was growing up was a savings account. "Put your money in a bank and let it draw interest," my teachers would tell me.

Today, those with money locked into 5 and 6 percent accounts are hurting; they are not keeping up with inflation. They are part of the Bible's group that "tendeth to poverty."

The Word says the man who is stingy, who hoards and clutches at the wealth he has, will soon become poor. It also says the man who gives his money away — the liberal soul — **shall be made fat**.

The Skeptic just fell off his chair again. "There you ago again, Brother John," he is saying, "trying to get me to give my money away — money I've worked hard to get, and I want to keep."

To dear Mr. Skeptic, and to you if you are like him, let me again remind you, this is not Brother John telling you these things. *It is the Word of God*!

God's Word is founded in generosity. Look at Luke 6:38: **Give, and it shall be given unto you....**

Both Old and New Testament scriptures say the same thing: as you are generous in all things, you will be prospered, fat, watered, and blessed. This is not a sales gimmick invented by some ministry to get you to participate in giving; this is God's guarantee, His Word, His promise to you.

He did not say to give to John Avanzini — and I am not telling you to do that. I am simply reporting the Word to you; it clearly says that for you to prosper, you need to be generous to those who are the storehouse and provide the meat of God's Word in your life. If my book and my television teachings provide you some of the meat you use in your spiritual walk, then by all means support this ministry; the Word tells you to do it in order to prosper. If this ministry does not provide that function in your life, then give to the ministry that does.

The devil, the father of the world, is greedy. He would have you be fearful and selfish. If you notice those characteristics associated with your own giving, then you need to kick the devil's lies out of your life and start believing the promises of God.

The Lord, the Father of the heaven, is always generous. His guarantees and promises are built on trust. He asks you to have your mind on others.

If you find yourself stingy in your finances when it comes to giving to God, it is because that "old man" is still in your habits; the old man of greed is still trying to dominate your life and deprive you of God's blessings.

Generosity is characteristic of God. When you are generous, it is God's personality beaming through you. As you sow liberally into God's field, He will see to it that you reap an abundant harvest for His glory.

In order to reap the harvest, every farmer needs to know the laws, the rules of nature concerning how to produce a crop. So, too, in the spiritual realm.

It is vital that you understand the Laws of Sowing.

Law Number One: Sowing brings reaping in kind.

How long do you think it would take for an apple tree to grow a peach? How many seasons would have to pass, how many years would roots need to grow, how many apples would have to fall to the ground, before the first peach started to grow? How long would it take for a carrot patch to produce the first fig? Like begets like. Sowing brings reaping in kind. No apple farmer will ever reap a harvest of peaches from his apple trees. No backyard gardener will ever see one carrot patch produce a fig.

Galatians 6:7 takes this natural law of God and puts it into very clear words: **Be not deceived; God is not mocked: for whatsoever a man soweth, that shall he also reap.** Listen to what the Word says here. Our Lord will not be mocked! The Word warns us not to be fooled. If you plant apples, expect apples. If you plant carrots, expect carrots. **...whatsoever a man soweth, that shall he also reap.**

"Why, I know that...that's no big deal in my book," shouts the Skeptic. Yes, Skeptic, you do understand this important Biblical principle when it is stated obviously with apples and carrots. But what about other areas? Did you ever stop to think that this law applies to finances, to love relationships, to fellow workers as well?

If you sow friendship, then you can expect the same law will return friendship to you. If you sow hatred to others in your work atmosphere, then hatred will be returned to you. And if you are stingy in your finances with God then how can money be returned to you?

God is not mocked! Each time I smile, I can expect to receive a smile in return. When I frown, I had better be prepared to see an ugly face. I always get back what I plant.

Now, think very carefully, because this is where people's thinking starts to get confused. So often some sweet little lady will come up to me and say: "Brother John, I just don't understand God. I spend a lot of time at the church helping others and doing chores, but I don't experience God's abundance. I am always broke. Why doesn't God love me? I follow His rules and don't lie or cheat, yet I am always broke. What is wrong?"

The problem is in not understanding God's law. *Like begets like.*

If I ask this person: "Do you have many people helping *you*?" her answer will be an enthusiastic "Yes." If I ask this person: "Do many people lie to you?" she would respond, "No, almost never."

You see, she is reaping what she sows. Her helping reaps helping. Her truthfulness reaps truth. If she wants money, she needs to plant money. Like begets like.

To apply this principle in your own life, you need only to ask yourself one very simple question: "What do I have a lack of?"

If you have a lack of love, start loving others, and you will have more love than you think you can handle. If your bills are getting too large, don't do what the world says and hoard what little you have; instead, do what God says and give some of your money away, plant some seed money to reap a money harvest.

You cannot sow money and expect to receive love. You cannot sow love and expect to receive money.

Whatever seed you put into the ground will yield that particular fruit, and no other. Like begets like.

Law Number Two: Reaping is in proportion to sowing.

But this I say, He which soweth sparingly shall reap also sparingly; and he which soweth bountifully shall reap also bountifully.

2 Corinthians 9:6

This truth is so simple that the shocking implications it contains are easily overlooked. Before you read one word further, go back to Second Corinthians 9:6 and read it out loud at least five times, asking God to teach your spirit what He would have you know about this verse.

His principles will not change. If you are a person who is not liberal to others, God will not change His whole plan just to accommodate you. The amount of love, the amount of money, the amount of friendship you receive is *decided by you*!

As you sow sparingly, you will reap sparingly. As you sow bountifully, you will reap bountifully.

I told you earlier that there are some shocking implications of this verse. One shocking implication is: *God is not moved by need*!

On a spiritual shock scale from one to ten, this is an eleven! When God sees that you need something, He will not necessarily move. If God were moved only by the need, then He would move primarily in India, in Mexico, and in Africa — where the needs are obvious and great.

When I first heard this concept, it caused me great pain. I thought God certainly must be moved by need. (He cares about the need, but is not always moved to action.) If He were moved by need, then the only places He would move would be in the lives of needy people.

Yet we have whole nations who sleep in the streets. How can this be? God moves *where there is a seed*, not just a need.

God says if you have a need — a lack you want to turn into a harvest — then you must first plant a seed from that lack in order to begin to reap. Faith in God's promises involves an *act*, a seed planting to release the process of harvest in your own life.

When Jesus walked the face of this earth, who were the people He answered, who were the people who had their needs met? Those who stepped out in faith and *acted first*. The sick were healed by acting in faith and touching His garment. They planted the seed of faith and believed for their healing, and they were healed.

Jesus walked past many people who could not see. Jesus left many sick people in their beds to die. Jesus encountered countless lepers with sores left open. Why? Because He did not care? Of course not.

These people were not touched by Jesus because He was bound by the *Biblical principle of sowing*: the seed must be planted first. The blind had to reach out, the sick had to touch His garment...each miracle first needed a seed to be planted before Jesus was free to respond.

If you have a need, and have been asking God: "Lord, why don't you see that I have a need?" then, you need to know He will not operate in violation to his Biblical law. You must turn your need into seed *before* you can begin to reap your personal harvest.

The person who needs to give the most today is the person who needs the most. The person who suffers from a life devoid of love needs to start planting lots of love.

The same book that says in John 3:16, **For God so loved the world, that he gave his only begotten Son, that whosoever believeth in him should not perish, but have everlasting life**, also says: **But this I say, He which soweth sparingly shall reap also sparingly; and he which soweth bountifully shall reap also bountifully** (2 Cor. 9:6).

Many Christians want to use the Bible as they do a grocery store, simply wandering through it picking and selecting only those things that meet their hunger. You cannot stand on one verse and toss out another.

Praise God, whatever you need, it can be met! You can put an immediate stop to any need simply by beginning to sow whatever you lack — the precious seed of which you have only a small amount — in order for God's law to begin to reap a harvest.

Law Number Three: Sow in all seasons.

> **He that observeth the wind shall not sow; and he that regardeth the clouds shall not reap.**
>
> **In the morning sow thy seed, and in the evening withhold not thine hand: for thou knowest not whether shall prosper, either this or that, or whether they both shall be alike good.**
>
> **Ecclesiastes 11:4,6**

So often I hear someone say: "When the Lord blesses me with a large amount of money [they usually quote some ridiculous figure, like a million dollars] I will give Him back at least half of it. But right now, I just can't afford to give anything."

Do not look at the wind, do not look at the circumstances in your life and expect them to change without action, without seed planting on your part now. God tells you in the verses above to plant your seeds — no matter what kind of weather you are having. If you are waiting for perfect conditions before you give to God, you will never give anything.

If a farmer goes out each day and notices a cloud or a bit of wind and decides not to plant, he will never have a crop. Conditions are *never* perfect. Some seed will be blown away by the wind, some seed will be eaten by the birds, and some seed will be buried too deep in the ground. But much seed will take root and produce harvest. You need to put seed out all the time so that some will find fertile ground and abundantly produce a harvest.

If you plant a garden in your backyard, you expect a miracle. Farmers know that a little seed, thrown on the ground and covered up, will produce the miracle of germination, and a crop much larger than the seed will result. The small package you buy to plant your garden results in a harvest much larger than several grocery bags of food.

So too, people who plant seed money in the Gospel of God should expect miracles of germination. God can take your dollar bill, your seed, and multiply it in the Gospel and win someone in Africa to Christ. God can take your ten dollar bill, your seed, and multiply it in the Gospel to help produce an hour television show for His glory. Just as surely as you know one tiny seed can bring forth a huge tree, you should know that your contribution, whatever the size of the seed, when planted in the work of the Gospel, will produce huge spiritual trees, larger than any you have ever seen in the natural realm.

Sow in all seasons. Pay no attention to the circumstances of your life. If you have abundance, sow. If your house payment is due, sow. If you have just received a large raise, sow. Pay no attention to the weather in your life.

"But you don't know how bad my circumstances are! Sometimes things just get so bad I have to cry."

I love you in the Lord. I would not tell you these things or report to you what the Word of God says unless I practiced the principles in my own life, and unless I deeply believed they would work in yours.

In fact, it is more than my belief! It is God's Word! If your circumstances are currently bad, then more than ever you need to sow. Read Psalm 126:5,6:

> **They that sow in tears shall reap in joy.**

> **He that goeth forth and weepeth, bearing precious seed, shall doubtless come again with rejoicing, bringing his sheaves with him.**

Even if you are in tears from your circumstances, the Word says sow and you "shall reap in joy." But this passage means more than that. It also refers to your concern for others. As you give your gift to the Gospel, you release that sowing with concern, with tears, with prayers for those to whom it is given.

There are a lot of Christians who send in their five or ten dollars to a ministry, but forget the *tears*, the concern. God expects you also to pray as you carry forth your *precious seed*.

Two very important things happen when prayer comes with your seed gift:

1. Your prayer creates an effectual door for the spending of the money you send. When your church or other gospel ministry receives it, their prayer combined with your prayer gives your seed a spiritual elevation. Unless the anointing of God is upon the funds of a ministry, all the money in the world would not bring about one person's salvation.

2. When your seed gift is watered with the tears of prayer, it can only grow faster, higher, taller, and stronger. Your gift, combined with your prayers and the prayers of others throughout the world, is so well cultivated that it can only produce fruit.

The next time you prepare your Sunday church envelope, remember to lay hands on it, to pray over it. The next time you send money to your favorite parachurch ministry, do not send it without first anointing it in prayer, so you can **come again...rejoicing, bringing sheaves with you** (Ps. 126:6).

13

Trust Your Man of God

Satan knows something about Biblical economics that most Christians do not know. He knows if you do not trust your man of God, you have disqualified yourself from operating in the miracle of God's prosperity. The Bible says:

> **And they rose early in the morning, and went forth into the wilderness of Tekoa; and as they went forth, Jehoshaphat stood and said, Hear me, O Judah, and ye inhabitants of Jerusalem; Believe in the Lord your God, so shall ye be established;** *believe his prophets, so shall ye prosper*.
>
> **2 Chronicles 20:20**

As long as the devil can keep God's children from trusting the men and women of God with their finances, he has them where he wants them. The Bible says without trust in the fivefold ministry, there can be no prosperity from God.

No single segment of society is more unfairly treated than gospel preachers. No other profession — not bankers, doctors, lawyers, politicians, white collar, blue collar, skilled or unskilled — are so unjustly judged. All preachers are forced to bear the reputation of the worst preachers.

Scandals are rampant in every profession in our nation. Hundreds of banks have gone bankrupt. The nation's leading newspaper recently reported that almost every one of these bankruptcies involved some form of fraud on the part of the bankers. Even with these hundreds of charlatan bankers, no one in his right mind would say that all bankers want is your money.

More and more frequently we see school teachers going on strike. They refuse to teach our children unless we pay them more money. Yet, no rational person would say that all school teachers want is your money.

Doctors and the medical profession have enjoyed greater price increases for their services than any segment of the economy. More people are stripped of their assets by medical bills than by any other means. Hospitals routinely refuse admittance to the injured until they can show proof of their ability to pay. As greedy as some of this seems, the general public is not saying that all doctors, nurses, and hospitals want is your money.

Something is very wrong. Everywhere you go, from nation to nation, you hear it spoken, "All preachers want is your money."

Preachers never go on strike. They are very seldom convicted of fraud. Their average pay scale is among the lowest in the nation. There has never been even one case of a preacher refusing to preach until he saw proof that the congregation could pay for the sermon.

Satan is deceiving the whole world into believing that *all preachers want is your money.*

> ...Satan...deceiveth the whole world....
> **Revelation 12:9**

Not only has he deceived the lost world, but he is succeeding in fooling most church members on this matter. Do not think Satan cannot fool a church member!

> ...if it were possible, they shall deceive the very elect.
>
> Matthew 24:24

The great miracles of God usually depend upon believing and trusting in the man of God. Let me begin the Biblical examination of this truth with an illustration from Second Kings 4. In the beginning of the chapter, we find a widow woman who was faced with a compound tragedy.

First, her husband had died. Next, she found that he had used her two sons as collateral for a debt he had made. The creditor had come to take her sons. Last of all, she was without the basic necessities of life. All she had left after the bankruptcy sale was a small pot of oil.

According to the text, it seems as if her own life had not been pledged against the debt. The pot of oil and her freedom were her only collateral. She could have tried to borrow her way out of debt by pledging her own life. The creditor probably would have extended her time to repay knowing that in a short while he would have her and her sons as servants.

How foolish we are when we think we can borrow our way out of debt. It would amaze you to know the number of God's people who are convinced that a nice, big loan would solve all their problems. Please don't misunderstand me. I am not saying Christians should never borrow money. I am saying that *more debt* is not the answer to *unmanageable debt*. Sooner or later, your debt must be *faced and paid off*.

This widow was in trouble, but she was not without hope. The Bible says she had a little pot of oil.

> **...Thine handmaid hath not any thing in the house, save a pot of oil.**
>
> **2 Kings 4:2**

How much could her pot of oil have been worth? Maybe it was worth a few cents, or a dollar or two at the most. That's not much against a debt large enough to send a widow's two sons into slavery. However, *the value of anything is not established by the appraiser. The value is established by what it is used for.*

For instance, hand-carved rosewood furniture is among the world's most expensive. I have seen rosewood desks in Taiwan that sold for tens of thousands of dollars. They are appraised to be of tremendous value. However, if one of these desks were chopped up and burned in the fireplace, it would not be worth more than a few dollars a cord. Its use establishes its value.

Four pennies will not buy much. Even in the days of Jesus, it was barely 25 percent of a day's pay for a Roman soldier. However, once when it was all that a widow woman had, Jesus declared it to be worth more than the largest sums of money given into the treasury that day.

> **And he called unto him his disciples, and saith unto them, verily I say unto you, that *this poor widow hath cast more in than all they which have cast into the treasury.***
>
> **Mark 12:43**

The way she used her few pennies established their value.

The little pot of oil the widow had did not sound like much, but notice how she used it. She made it available to God. That one fact greatly enhanced its worth.

Beyond this oil, this widow had one more asset. She had an asset most millionaires do not have. She had a man of God she could trust *with the last thing she had*. She did not think that all her man of God wanted was her money. When Elisha asked her what she had in her house, she did not lie to him. She did not have to act as if she forgot about the oil.

The Bible suggests that the creditor had already cleaned out her home. The man of God asked her what she had. It was a strong question to ask, especially of a widow who had just had all her goods sold at a public auction. What great faith Elisha had in God's Word. How do you ask a widow what she has left after the auction of her goods?

Her house was empty except for one little pot of oil that no one had bid on. When Elisha heard this, he gave her some very strange instructions. He told her to borrow empty vessels.

Now, just think a moment. Who would lend anything to this bankrupt widow? How could she ask to borrow from her neighbors when they were aware of her total insolvency? Most people would have politely excused themselves and walked away. However, this woman was not like most people. She was unique, a peculiar person, for she could believe in her man of God. She did as he commanded her and asked to borrow vessels of her neighbors.

Once she gathered the empty vessels, she obeyed Elisha, brought them into her house, and closed the doors and windows. I did not understand the significance of these instructions for many years. At first I thought God wanted to shield the miracle of multiplication from the prying eyes of her neighbors. After meditating on this, I had to change my mind. This would not be consistent with the way God performed other miracles. His miracles were usually performed out in the open for everyone to see.

Then one day while reading Second Corinthians I found the reason Elisha insisted that she have some privacy. I read that Paul had instructed those who took offerings never to put pressure on people to give more than they really wanted to give.

> **Every one must make up his own mind as to how much he should give.** *Don't force anyone to give more than he really wants to*, **for cheerful givers are the ones God prizes.**
>
> **2 Corinthians 9:7** TLB

This woman was given total privacy. No pressure was put on her in any way by the man of God. He gave her clear instructions to pour the little pot of oil into the many vessels she had borrowed. He then sent her into a closed house to see the oil multiplied.

Notice that Elisha never once mentioned to this woman what she would be asked to do with the oil after it was multiplied. This was not necessary, for she trusted her man of God!

If she believed that Elisha's only interest was in her oil, she never would have told him she had it. If she did not trust Elisha, she would have hidden a few barrels of the multiplied oil, just in case he would want too much for himself. Either of these acts of distrust would have immediately canceled her miracle, for you must believe the prophets in order to prosper. (2 Chronicles 20:20.)

We find this woman totally trusted her man of God. We also find that her man of God was not after her money. He was first and foremost dedicated to the elimination of her debt.

> **Then she came and told the man of God. And he said, Go, sell the oil, and *pay the debt*, and live thou and thy children of the rest.**
>
> **2 Kings 4:7**

Most people are only impressed with the miracle of the multiplication of the little pot of oil. This was a great miracle, but I suggest that it was not the greatest miracle of this event. The entire world supply of olive oil is multiplied every year. It is a common miracle of nature.

The greatest miracle I find here is that this widow had enough confidence in her man of God to trust him with the *last thing she had*. The loose talkers of her day had not spoiled her confidence in him. She knew he had a higher interest in her life than getting her money.

Read the account carefully. It will reveal Elisha's motive. You will find that he did not even ask her for the tithe on her miracle increase. He did not ask her for an offering. He simply told her to sell the oil, pay her debt, and live off the rest. With that said, the account closes. Elisha was interested in meeting her need, not his.

However, I am convinced that she did tithe and give offerings to God from her increase. It stands to reason that this widow who trusted God with the last thing she had would give God the modest portion of her increase He required.

There is a *second* case of a woman trusting her man of God and how this trust opened the provision of God to her.

There was a very special widow woman who lived in Zarephath. We know she was a very special woman because God visited with her in a very special way. First Kings, chapter 17, tells us of her personal encounter with God. Upon close examination of the text, we can conclude that He actually manifested Himself to her. He gave her specific instructions concerning the prophet, Elijah.

And the word of the Lord came unto him (Elijah), **saying,**

Arise, get thee to Zarephath, which belongeth to Zidon, and dwell there: behold, *I have commanded a widow woman there to sustain thee.*

1 Kings 17:8,9

Upon Elijah's arrival at Zarephath, he saw the woman out in the field gathering sticks. As he approached her, he did not know she was down to her last bit of food. When he saw her, he boldly asked her to feed him.

...Bring me, I pray thee, a morsel of bread in thine hand.

1 Kings 17:11

This should not have caused her to react, for God had told her to sustain him. However, her response was far from what would be expected. When the woman heard these words, her heart was gripped with *fear.* She spontaneously cried out with an oath that she and her son were at starvation's door.

> ...As the Lord thy God liveth, I have not a cake, but an handful of meal in a barrel, and a little oil in a cruse: and, behold, I am gathering two sticks, that I may go in and dress it *for me and my son, that we may eat it, and die.*
>
> 1 Kings 17:12

No doubt this angry response caught Elijah off guard. After all, he knew God had commanded her to feed him. Thank God for the discernment of the true man of God. Elijah immediately saw that the fear of insufficiency had gripped her, and he began to minister to her.

> And Elijah said unto her, *fear not....*
>
> 1 Kings 17:13

The simple fact was that fear had caused this woman to disobey her God. The Bible clearly states that fear does not come from God.

> For God hath *not* given us the *spirit of fear....*
>
> 2 Timothy 1:7

Whenever a child of God walks in fear, he is immediately exposed to the torment of the devil.

> ...*fear* hath *torment....*
>
> 1 John 4:18

Try to imagine the torment of this poor widow. It was so great she was disobeying God and thereby sealing the doom of herself and her son. She was eliminating her only hope of overcoming her need. If she persisted in fear, she and her son would be dead in a few days.

Even in her fright-induced disobedience, she still held the key to the storehouse of God. A little cake was all that stood between her and starvation. *She trusted her man of God enough to give him the last thing she had.*

Immediately upon releasing the little cake to Elijah, God released the miracle of abundant supply to her. The barrel of meal began to refill itself, and the pot of oil miraculously increased in volume. Because she could trust her man of God, she and her son survived the famine. Her attitude toward Elijah had not been affected by those who tried to tell her all he wanted was her money. She cast down the evil imaginations of her day and moved into God's best.

> ...believe his prophets, so shall ye prosper.
> 2 Chronicles 20:20

Let me show you the third case of a person who trusted his man of God and received financial deliverance. This time I want to discuss an event that happened between Simon Peter and Jesus. The story is found in Matthew 17.

The account opens with a tax collector at the door. He was there to collect taxes from our Lord and His disciple, Peter. Jesus gave Simon Peter instructions on how to receive a financial miracle to pay their taxes.

> ...go thou to the sea, and cast an hook, and take up the fish that first cometh up; and when thou hast opened his mouth, thou shalt find *a piece of money*: that take, and give unto them *for me and thee*.
> Matthew 17:27

Think about these instructions a moment. Simon Peter was a fisherman. He had looked into the mouths of hundreds of thousands of fish, but he had never once found any money in a fish's mouth. It would have been easy for him to think, "There is no use looking in the fish's mouth for money. I've never found any money in a fish before."

If Simon Peter had not trusted his man of God, he might have ended up in debtors' prison. However, he had complete trust in Jesus Christ, his man of God. He went to the sea, cast in the hook, and found the coin. With it he paid the Lord's tax and his own.

These are three tremendous illustrations from God's Word. They prove beyond a shadow of doubt that the prosperity of God hinges on a trust relationship with your man of God.

Your pastor is your man of God. If you have had doubts about him, *cast them down*. If you have heard rumors about him that disturb your confidence in him, *reject them*. If you have heard a bad report about some other man of God, do not let it taint your thinking about your pastor.

Your favorite missionary is your man of God. Your evangelist is your man of God. The apostles and prophets God has sent into your life are your men of God. Do not let the gainsayers break your trust in them.

There may be other men and women of God in your life. The person who led you to the Lord may be one of them. There may be a television or radio preacher, or a Christian writer who ministers to you. All of these are prophets in your life.

You must keep the lies of the devil from separating you from them. Do not stop trusting these chosen vessels, for if you do, you will stop the prosperity of God in your life.

> ...believe his prophets, so shall ye prosper.
> 2 Chronicles 20:20

How easily we fall into the patterns of the world. How quickly we stop trusting the men and women of God. Make up your mind that you are going to safeguard your relationship with your man of God.

The widow who was left with a great debt believed her prophet, and her entire debt was paid, plus enough to retire on. This happened primarily because she trusted her man of God with the last bit of oil she had.

The widow at Zarephath was saved from starvation because she could trust her man of God with the last bit of food in the house.

Simon Peter paid his taxes and avoided debtors' prison because he believed his man of God. Even when he knew no fish had ever before come out of the sea with a coin in its mouth, in faith he obeyed Jesus.

A country-Western singer once had a best-selling record. It was called, "Stand by Your Man." It was one of the few secular songs with a positive message. I challenge Christian song writers to write a song entitled, "Stand by Your Man of God."

> ...believe his prophets, so shall ye prosper.
> 2 Chronicles 20:20

14

What Not To Do in Recession

Many of the things you have read in this book are completely new ideas, and by now, I believe you are grasping in your spirit that the Word of God deals with all of your life — your health, your finances, your prayer, your spirit.

The Word of God serves as a guide for solving your problems, a guide for getting your promotion. In this chapter I want to show you certain guidelines for behavior that the Bible outlines for the hard times, the famine in your life.

The first clear statement the Bible makes concerning famine (today, we would say hard times, depression, runaway inflation, and so on) is: *Don't go down to Egypt!*

We saw earlier that Isaac was faced with a decision in his life:

a. He could stay and sow in famine, or

b. He could go down to Egypt.

Isaac decided to stay where he was and obey God. He had faith in God's word, and obeyed by sowing in drought.

> **And the Lord appeared unto him, and said, Go not down into Egypt; dwell in the land which I shall tell thee of.**
>
> **Genesis 26:2**

Egypt represents the things of the world in our day. God warns us not to dwell in the place, the mental attitude, of the world, but to dwell in the land He has for us.

If you are believing the television commentators who constantly cry about the gloom of the day, then start to hear the voice of God instead of the voice of man. Remember, these same fellows who tell you how bad things become each day are the same people who give bad advice about handling your money. You know by now how that works!

So look to the Word. When the world tells you to stop giving because "times are tight," then you *stay out of Egypt*! Pay no attention to the cries and shouts of gloom and doom, but do as Isaac did and sow in faith in the midst of drought. God will honor His Word, His promise, and will bring a personal harvest into your life.

We are down to the final days — the time when you either do what the world says or you do what God says. The world says when your business is going slow, stop giving to God. That may kill your business or cost you your job.

God tells us that if we are experiencing financial difficulties, it is probably because we are not giving enough to His purposes. If you bring tithes into His storehouse, He guarantees He will open the windows of heaven over your life. If you give offerings, He will pour you out a blessing.

Stay out of Egypt! Do not listen to the gospel of the world. The gospel of the world is to keep all you can; the Gospel of Jesus Christ is one of generosity — of giving and receiving and reaping the harvest. No matter how bad it looks, sow your seeds in the land of God. Stay out of Egypt. The liberal soul shall be made fat.

The second clear statement the Bible makes concerning a famine is: *Don't eat up the seed corn.*

Look again at the widow of Zarephath in First Kings 17:12. There was famine in the land, and the poor woman had only enough food left for one meal. When Elijah asked her for some nourishment, her reply could easily be the reply of many of our widows on Social Security in this modern day:

> **And she said, As the Lord thy God liveth, I have not a cake, but an handful of meal in a barrel, and a little oil in a cruse: and, behold, I am gathering two sticks, that I may go in and dress (prepare) it for me and my son, that we may eat it, and die.**

The prophet Elijah told the woman not to worry, but to go ahead and make her cake and feed him, and that the Lord would provide for her needs.

She obeyed. She believed the Word of God as spoken through the prophet, and she fed Elijah. And how did God respond? Look at verse 15:

> **And she went and did according to the saying of Elijah; and she, and he, and her house, did eat many days.**

Suppose she had not obeyed God? Suppose that little old widow had listened to the voices of the world, and she had made that final cake for her and her son? She would have died.

Instead, she obeyed God and acted in faith. She did not eat the seed corn. As a result, she ate from that barrel until the famine was off the land. Praise God!

The same lesson is also in Proverbs 3:27,28:

Withhold not good from them to whom it is due, when it is in the power of thine hand to do it.

Say not unto thy neighbor, Go, and come again, and to morrow I will give; when thou hast it by thee.

The Bible teaches you not to withhold from others when you have it near you, and even if you are down to your last little bit, go ahead and start to plant seeds.

Do not eat up the seed corn. Plant some of it in the work of the Gospel; but by all means, for your own protection, do not sit and eat your last bit by yourself.

If you do not plant, how can God give anything back to you? Get hold of this truth. Before everything is gone, before you have no seed left to plant the garden, put some seed into the ground to start the process of God's abundant blessing in your life.

The way of the world would say to eat the last little bit yourself, to make it last. God's way is to plant the last little bit, allow Him to make it grow, so you and your family can eat until the famine is over!

The third thing not to do during hard times, during a recession is: *Do not reject the messenger of God.*

Our modern-day society has created a philosophy that is leading us into destruction, without any instructions on how to escape the final, fatal blow. Our world is being taught, encouraged, and educated to buy on credit. We are taught by the world's teachers to go on spending sprees where impulse buying is the key, with no view or thought to the next morning's bills.

When the bills get too high, and the income is too low, the tower of credit buying starts to come tumbling down on top of the anxious buyer, pushing him into despair and bankruptcy court.

Man is not listening to the Word of God, or to God's men, his messengers. If times are hard in your life right now, listen instead to the words of God, not the words of the credit card companies.

Do not share your money with the makers of hopelessly high interest; the Bible says to sow your seeds in the work of God, and share with your neighbor.

Listen carefully to the prophets God is bringing up in these last days. Read Second Chronicles 20:20 and receive 20/20 vision concerning the things of God:

Believe in the Lord your God, so shall ye be established; believe his prophets, so shall ye prosper.

The widow believed the prophet Elijah, and she prospered. Believe God's Word, and you will be established; He will take care of you. Listen to His prophets, and you will prosper!

Being established means that hard times will not harm you, will not destroy you. But the Word tells us we do not have to stop with simple survival.

We can prosper by listening to His prophets! Day after day, I teach on television God's laws and Word concerning money. I am not trying to raise money; I am trying to raise saints of God who can stand tall in the evil days coming and who have more than enough to take care of any problem that will come up.

Put these principles to work in your life. Because I am one of God's prophets, He has shown these things to me to help protect you and prosper you in the endtimes. As you listen and others listen to God's Word in these matters, I know there will be more than enough to sow into the Gospel to bring Christ to the four corners of the earth!

In Acts 27:9-11 we see Paul acting as a prophet of God, warning the ship's crew about the dangers of setting sail in a storm:

> **And** (Paul) **said unto them, Sirs, I perceive that this voyage will be with hurt and much damage, not only of the loading** (cargo) **and ship, but also of our lives.**
>
> **Acts 27:10**

The captain of the vessel did not listen. He knew from his worldly experience that the ship would be just fine, and that the ship would not sink. As a result, the ship and all the cargo were lost.

Do not reject the Word of God, God's message to you. Do not reject His messengers — modern-day prophets teaching what the Spirit of God shows them about the Word. Believe His prophets, and you will prosper.

The fourth thing not to do when times are hard is: *Don't think you cannot give because you do not have anything.*

Hannah was a very powerful woman of God, and because of her love for the Lord, she wanted to give a son to His service in the priesthood. She wanted her son to serve as a priest in the temple all the days of his life.

Unfortunately, she did not have a son to give to God. Even though year after year she was barren, this fact did not stop Hannah. She pledged her son-to-be in faith to God, believing He would give her a son. When He did, she would then give him back to God in the priesthood.

She gave a son she did not have, by faith, by her vow. In First Samuel 1:11, we read her beautiful prayer of faith.

> **And she vowed a vow, and said, O Lord of hosts, if thou wilt indeed look on the affliction of thine handmaid, and remember me, and not forget thine handmaid, but wilt give unto thine handmaid a man child, then I will give him unto the Lord all the days of his life, and there shall no razor come upon his head.**

Other women had sons to give to God in the priesthood, but not Hannah. So what did Hannah do? She told the Lord, "Give me a son, and I'll give him right back to you in the priesthood!"

Many of you find your checkbooks or refrigerators are barren. You have no food to give to a neighbor, and no money to plant into the work of the Lord. For many, even the cost of a stamp is too much. But in your heart, you want to give to God. As you have read this book, the Spirit has convicted you as to the truth of these teachings, and you now want to apply God's principles to your life.

If you are in a poverty cycle and want to break it, but you have nothing to give, do as Hannah did, and pledge your future fruit.

Believe God. Tell Him right now in prayer that if He will provide you with a sum of $5, $10, and so on, you will plant that seed money into the Gospel for His glory, and will begin to loose the poverty bondage now operating in your life.

You can give, even when you do not have money. God honors your heart, just as He honored Hannah's heart. Make a faith vow to the Lord, and never again think that you cannot give, because you do not have anything. That is the thinking of the world.

The final thing I want to talk about in this chapter that you *should not do* in recession is: *Do not try to reason your way out!*

If you have learned anything from this book, I would hope it is clear to you now that the ways of the world are not the ways of God. No longer do you have to rely on your own worldly reasoning to conquer your problems. No longer do you need to rely on the commentators you see and hear on television.

To stay out of recession, even when it is all around you, look to the Word of God, not to your own reasoning.

The world says to hoard your possessions; the Word says: **Give, and it shall be given unto you**. The world says it is crazy to give away 10 percent of your income; the Word says to tithe, and the very windows of heaven shall be open on your life.

The world says "can all you get;" but the Word says sow and you will reap.

The world has countless plans for profit: put your money into gold, into silver, into diamonds, into real estate, into stocks, into banks, and under your mattress; but the Word says to put your money into the Gospel and God will keep on multiplying it for His glory.

The ways of man are often reasonable, yet often lead to destruction. The way of the Word often defies the logic of the world, but always leads to prosperity and abundance!

In First Corinthians 1:19, we read:

> **For it is written, I will destroy the wisdom of the wise, and will bring to nothing the understanding of the prudent.**

In verse 27 of the same chapter, it further states:

> **But God hath chosen the foolish things of the world to confound the wise; and God hath chosen the weak things of the world to confound the things which are mighty.**

And finally, in First Corinthians 2:13,14, we are told to compare spiritual things with spiritual things — not with worldly matters.

> **Which things also we speak, not in the words which man's wisdom teacheth, but which the Holy Ghost teacheth; comparing spiritual things with spiritual.**

> **But the natural man receiveth not the things of the Spirit of God; for they are foolishness unto him: neither can he know them, because they are spiritually discerned.**

Do not try to reason with the world's wisdom! The world's philosophies are foolishness, and will not serve you in the faithful manner of the Word of God. God's Word will produce more blessings for you in five minutes than the wisdom of a man could in five centuries.

Let God's Word be your advisor during a recession. Do not lean on your own logic; stay out of the flesh and let the Spirit lead your decisions. Let the Spirit show you where to go during the day, and what to read and what to say. As you are open to His guidance, the Word guarantees that you will not only survive in recession, but you will prosper during it.

15

God Wants You To Prosper

By now, the very foundations of your traditional thoughts on giving, receiving, and prospering have been shaken free of the lies of Satan, and you are grasping the beautiful love of your great God: *God wants you to prosper*!

Third John 2 says:

Beloved, I wish *above all things* that thou mayest prosper and be in *health*, even as thy soul *prospereth*.

Did you hear that fantastic news? God wants you to prosper.

Notice the *high priority* He gives to your prospering. God wants it for you *above all things*! Above all things in the universe, God wants you to prosper. Above all things in the galaxy, God wants you to prosper. Even as God sustains all the molecules and matter in His magnificent creation, He has as *His primary desire, that you prosper*.

His prosperity is total. God wants to prosper you *mentally*; He wants you to be at peace.

Peace I leave you, peace I give unto you: not as the world giveth, give I unto you.
John 14:27

Notice your peace is already here, and in great abundance. Jesus said: *My peace I leave you*. Your peace is not way off somewhere in a distant land called heaven. It is right here and now! It is not in the future; grasp that. He said: **Peace I give unto you...**

The present tense. Your peace, your mental prosperity, is provided by your loving God *in the now*.

God also wants you to prosper physically — to be in good health, to have health in great abundance. He took on Himself cruel stripes that purchased health for all.

In Isaiah 53:5 we read: **...and with his stripes we are healed.** The present tense.

There is more than enough health for you, and it is provided by your loving God *in the now*.

God also wants you to prosper (present tense) in your finances. Look at Second Peter 1:3:

> **According as his divine power hath given unto us all things** (total, complete) **that pertain unto life....**

God desires that you prosper *financially*. He has already provided for your financial prosperity *in the now*.

All of this prosperity — mental, physical, and financial — *is yours now*! *But*, notice a critical condition: **...even as your soul prospers.**

God tells us to take care of the inner man, to be right with Him in all things.

Feed your inner man. Keep him on a good, healthy diet of God's Word. Place him on a good exercise program of doing God's will. Enroll him in a good mental hygiene program, thinking only about the good things of God. *Then*, as your soul prospers, *so, too*, will your health and finances.

Don't you just feel in your heart that as you draw nearer to the Lord, He will draw nearer to you? The Word says it is so in James 4:8.

Don't you just know that as you put this great body of truth about giving and receiving from God to work for you, your prosperity in the financial realm is already becoming a reality?

For those who flow in His will, the Bible clearly states it is *His desire* that you prosper. The two points are connected; your earthly prosperity as God's child is tied directly to your spiritual prosperity.

Remember in an earlier chapter, we discussed Deuteronomy 8:18:

> **But thou shalt remember the Lord thy God: for it is he that** *giveth thee power to get wealth*, **that he may establish his covenant which he sware unto thy fathers, as it is this day.**

God not only wants you to prosper, but He gives you the power to get wealth. For so long, I thought it was godly to be poor. For so long, I thought going without things was an act of contrition on my part, and somehow believed my dedication to poverty impressed God. But that is not what the Bible says.

He wants you to prosper, and He gives you the power to get wealth. God has a covenant with you. If you understand God and His Word, and if your life is one that abides in His will, then the Lord has a covenant of blessing for your life.

"But Brother John, you know, money is the root of all evil," Mr. Skeptic smugly shouts. "The Bible teaches that, you know."

Skeptic, hold on to your skeptical halo. The Word of God *does not say* that money is the root of all evil. In First Timothy 6:10 it reads:

> **For the love of money is the root of all evil, which, while some coveted after, they have erred from the faith, and pierced themselves through with many sorrows.**

The *love of money* is the root of all evil. If the money itself were evil, *God would not give you the power to obtain it*. He does promise that as His *obedient* child, you will receive plenty of wealth, as long as you do not develop a *love* for it.

The concepts in this book are so powerful that I cannot help but believe that if every child of God reading right now would believe and understand Deuteronomy 8:18 about God giving the power to get wealth, we could supply all the Christian ministry needs in the world today, and bring back the King in short order.

This is the whole purpose for God's giving us wealth; He expects us to spread His Word. Wealth derived for the wrong purpose would never make you happy. If it did, then no one with money would ever commit suicide or go into divorce court or have a drinking problem. Wealth not received from God will not make you happy. Many times people with the most money are also those with the most misery.

When wealth is obtained through God's Plan, it comes with the promise that it will make you happy — without sorrow. Proverbs 10:22 states:

> **The blessing of the Lord, it maketh rich, and he addeth no sorrow with it.**

What type of riches causes sorrow? The type we desperately try to hold on to, the riches that mean so much to us that their loss would be a major crisis in life.

God's wealth is different. It is a wealth *to be given away*!

Once again we see that God's wisdom is foolishness in the world. Givers get, to give again — to Him, for His glory.

If it were not for the greed of man, there would be more than enough abundance on earth. There is more than enough money on earth right now for every man, woman, boy and girl to live like a millionaire! That's right, all four and a half *billion* people on this earth could live like millionaires were it not for the greed of man!

As you start receiving from God as you apply His laws, do not let greed get in the way of His purpose. As you receive, turn right around and give a generous measure back into His ministries. Give the tithe; get those windows of heaven open in your life. Give great, generous offerings to those places God tells you to, so that a good measure will be poured out to you through the open windows of heaven.

Be careful that the abundance of your life does not start to make you greedy. Let God shine through all of your life, especially through your financial matters. The only wealth that will not bring sorrow is the wealth that you control, the wealth that does not control you, wealth *you do not love*, but are willing to put back into the Gospel of God.

Ecclesiastes 10:19 says ...**money answereth all things**. Is your money doing that? Is your money building God's Kingdom or building your kingdom? Remember Luke 6:38:

> **Give, and it shall be given unto you; good measure, pressed down, and shaken together, and running over, shall men give into your bosom. For with the same measure that ye mete** (measure), **it shall be measured to you again.**

Remember, there is more than enough for the man or woman who is a gracious giver, and by putting the principles you have just read into practice, you, too, can soon be always abounding in the good things of God.

Dr. John F. Avanzini was born in Paramaribo, Surinam, South America, in 1936. He was raised and educated in Texas, and received his doctorate in philosophy from Baptist Christian University, Shreveport, Louisiana. Dr. Avanzini now resides with his wife, Pat, in Fort Worth, Texas, where he is the Director of His Image Ministries.

Dr. Avanzini's television program, *Principles of Biblical Economics,* is aired five times per day, seven days per week, by more than 550 television stations from coast to coast. He speaks nationally and internationally in conferences and seminars every week. His tape and book ministry is worldwide, and many of his vibrant teachings are now available in tape and book form.

Dr. Avanzini is an extraordinary teacher of the Word of God, bringing forth many of the present truths that God is using in these days to prepare the body of Christ for His triumphant return.

To contact Dr. Avanzini, write:

Dr. John F. Avanzini
P. O. Box 1057
Hurst, Texas 76053

*Please include your prayer requests
and comments when you write.*

Other Books by John Avanzini

Faith Extenders

30-60-Hundredfold

Powerful Principles of Increase

Rapid Debt-Reduction Strategies

Stolen Property Returned

War On Debt

The Wealth of the World

**Available from
your local bookstore,
or from**

Harrison House
P. O. Box 35035
Tulsa, OK 74153